Pies

KT-367-257

Pies

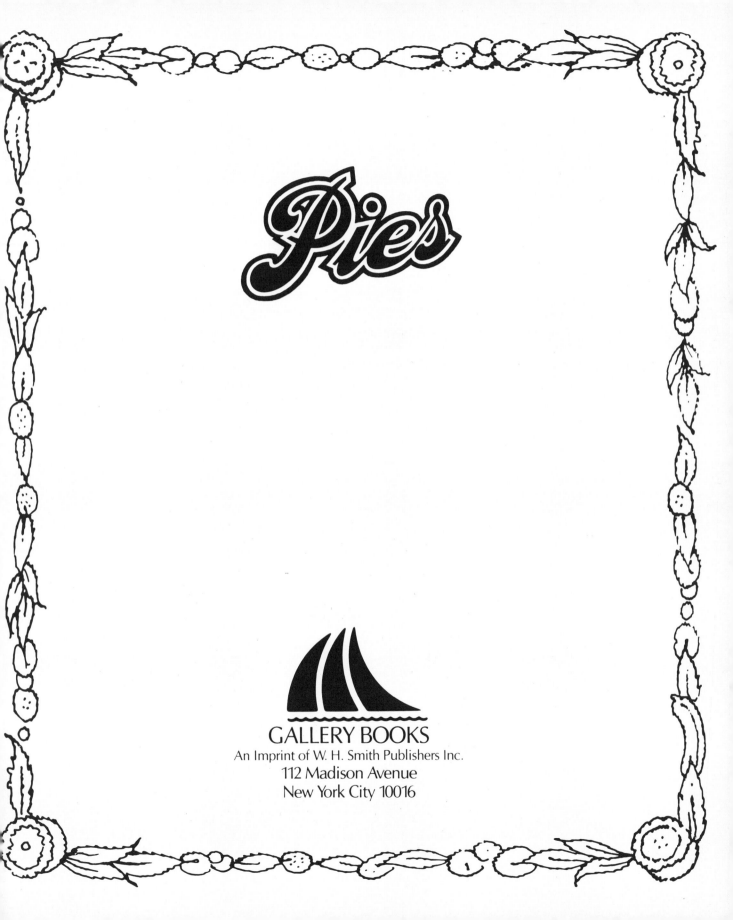

GALLERY BOOKS
An Imprint of W. H. Smith Publishers Inc.
112 Madison Avenue
New York City 10016

Editor: Annabel McLaren
Art editor: Caroline Dewing
Production: Richard Churchill
Illustrations and hand lettering: Ian Beck

Published by
GALLERY BOOKS
An imprint of W.H. Smith Publishers Inc.
112 Madison Avenue, New York,
New York 10016

© Marshall Cavendish Limited 1986

All rights reserved.

Printed and bound in Italy

ISBN 0 8317 1801-3

Contents

Introduction

Savory pies, made from a wide variety of tasty fillings, are among the most versatile of dishes. From attractive quiches to luxurious deep dish pies full of meaty goodness, in Country Kitchen Pies you will find a range of mouth-watering recipes. Whether you want to make an appetizing TV dinner or a midweek family meal, pack up a picnic or entertain friends in style, there are pies in this book that are sure to become firm favorites.

We've chosen a range of hearty pies for cold, wintry days when a warm, filling dish is needed and contrasted these with delicate, melt-in-the-mouth creations, perfect for serving chilled on hot summer days.

Making a pie gives the cook a chance to be really creative. A piecrust can be decorated as elaborately as your skills will allow, and even the most inexperienced can produce a glazed piecrust with a crisp, golden sheen that looks really professional. Pies are definitely as satisfying to make as they are to eat!

Country Kitchen Pies is divided into four at-a-glance sections. There are Top Crust Pies for filling main meals; Open-Faced Pies – including a range of quiches – for picnics, summer meals, buffets and parties; Double Crusts – including packages, turnovers and braids – for lunch and supper; and finally, Individual Pies, for just about any occasion.

The Dough

Most of the pies in this book can be made using either Basic pie dough or Puff pastry. You can, of course, cheat and use store-bought pastry but it is much more satisfying and infinitely more successful to make your own the Country Kitchen way. Follow the simple step-by-step directions and even preparing the notoriously difficult puff pastry will be a cinch.

Basic pie dough

This type of dough is made with half as much fat, by weight, as flour. A combination of half butter and half chilled leaf lard is best; the butter gives a rich color and flavor while the lard gives a deliciously "short" or tender texture. You can use shortening instead of butter if you prefer. The fats should be cold and firm, but not rock hard or they will be difficult to cut in. Always use a soft all-purpose flour and add a pinch of salt for flavor – even if the dish is to be a sweet one. Avoid self-rising flour which gives a crumbly dough.

Preparing the dough

Before you begin, get organized. Set out the ingredients, measure the water and chill it. If your hands are warm and sticky, cool them under a cold running faucet and dry them thoroughly.

To make the dough light and crisp you must incorporate as much air as possible. This is easy if you follow a few basic rules:

• always sift the flour, even if you have bought presifted flour.

• cut the fats into the flour quickly and work them in deftly with a pastry blender or with the tips of your fingers, lifting your fingertips well above the bowl.

• the texture of the cut-in mixture should resemble coarse meal or bread crumbs. It is the tiny pockets of fat in the flour that make the dough crisp and flaky so some cooks prefer to have quite large fat particles – around the size of peas or small beans.

• add only enough water to make the cut-in mixture cling together. For basic pie dough 1 tablespoon water to each cup of flour is usually sufficient but you may need more as flours vary in the amount of liquid they absorb. Too much water makes the dough sticky and hard to roll, too little produces a dry crumbly dough.

• handle the dough as lightly as possible; if it is overworked the fats become oily and the dough will be tough.
• keep the dough cool.

Puff pastry

A classic homemade puff pastry is unbeatable for melt-in-the-mouth texture and unforgettable flavor. Puff pastry is made in much the same way as its country cousins, rough puff and flaky pastry – by repeated rollings and foldings of the dough to trap air between the layers – but unlike the other puff pastries, this one uses equal amounts by weight of fat and flour and the method for incorporating the fat is different. It is this that gives the pastry its high-rise quality. Follow some basic rules for good results.

• work in cool surroundings – on a very hot day it helps if you use a fan to cool the air, but do not direct it onto your working surface.
• always sift the flour, even if it is presifted.
• if possible, use flour which has a high gluten content (bread flour). If this is difficult to obtain, all-purpose flour will do, but not self-rising which contains chemical leaveners.
• use a little chilled leaf lard at the start, then incorporate butter or firm shortening during the rolling and folding process. Butter gives the best flavor but shortening may be used if it is not the whipped variety. The butter needs to be the same consistency as the dough. Let it stand at room temperature until it is workable but still cool.
• bind the dough with ice water to which lemon juice has been added – this strengthens the flour.
• observe all the chilling times as outlined in the recipe.
• try not to let the pastry tear as this will release the air you've taken such care to trap between the layers.
• always chill and then bake in a hot oven, preheated to the exact temperature stipulated in the recipes.

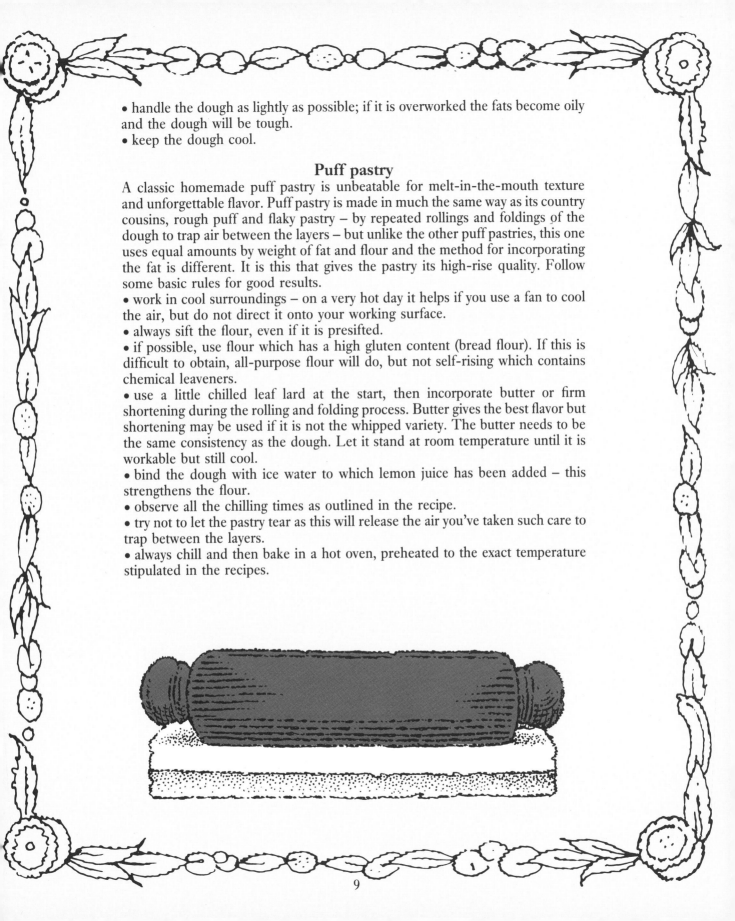

Basic pie dough

Makes about ¾ lb

2 cups all-purpose flour
pinch of salt
¼ cup butter or shortening
¼ cup chilled leaf lard
about ⅓–½ cup ice water

1 Sift the flour and salt into a large wide mixing bowl. Cut the fats in ½ inch cubes and add them to the flour.
2 Using the tips of your fingers and thumbs pick up a small amount of the mixture. Raise your hands well above the bowl and lightly rub thumbs over fingertips, letting the mixture trickle back into the bowl.
3 Continue rubbing the fats into the flour, working quickly, until all the mixture resembles particles of coarse meal or bread crumbs.
4 Sprinkle three-fourths of the ice water over the surface and mix it in with a knife. Using one hand, draw the mixture together. If it feels too dry, add the remaining water.
5 When the mixture clings together, lightly press it into a soft ball. Wrap the dough in aluminum foil and chill it in the refrigerator for at least 30 minutes before using as directed in the recipes that follow.

Puff pastry

Makes about 1¼ lb

2 cups high-gluten bread or all-purpose white flour
pinch of salt
2 tablespoons chilled leaf lard
½–¾ cup ice water
1 teaspoon lemon juice
¾ cup lightly salted butter

1 Sift the flour and salt into a bowl. Cut in the leaf lard and rub it in with your fingertips. Make a well in the center.

2 Mix ¼ cup ice water with the lemon juice and pour into the well. Mix with a fork to give a soft but not sticky dough, adding the remaining water if you find this necessary.

3 Place the dough on a lightly floured surface and knead it swiftly until smooth. Wrap the dough in plastic wrap or foil and chill in the refrigerator for 30 minutes.

4 Meanwhile place the butter between 2 sheets of waxed paper and beat it out with a rolling pin to a rectangle about 6 × 4 inches and around ½ inch thick.

5 On a lightly floured surface, roll out the dough to a 10 inch square. Peel the top piece of waxed paper off the butter, invert the butter on the center of the dough and peel off the remaining paper.

6 Fold the dough over the long sides of the butter so they slightly overlap and press seam gently to seal. Fold the short ends in to enclose the butter completely, then press again to seal.

7 Position the dough so that one of the short sides is toward you. Press the rolling pin gently down on the dough in 3 or 4 places to flatten it slightly, then roll out to a rectangle ¾ inch thick and 24 inches long and 8 inches wide (it should be 3 times as long as it is wide). Roll lightly and evenly away from you and do not take the rolling pin over the edges of the dough.

8 With the back of a knife, mark out the dough crosswise into 3 equal portions. Fold the bottom third over the center, then bring the top third over both. Seal the edges with a roller.

9 Turn the dough around so that a short side now faces you. Roll out to a rectangle again as in Step 7, but make each side of the rectangle about 1 inch shorter. If necessary, press a ruler against the edges of the pastry to keep them straight and to make the corners neat. Repeat Step 8. Wrap in plastic wrap and chill in the refrigerator for 30 minutes.

10 Repeat Steps 7–9 twice more (to make 6 rollings and foldings in all), reducing the size of the rectangle by around ½ inch on each edge at each rolling, but still keeping it 3 times as long as it is wide. After the final folding, wrap in plastic wrap and chill for at least 4 hours before using as directed in the recipes that follow.

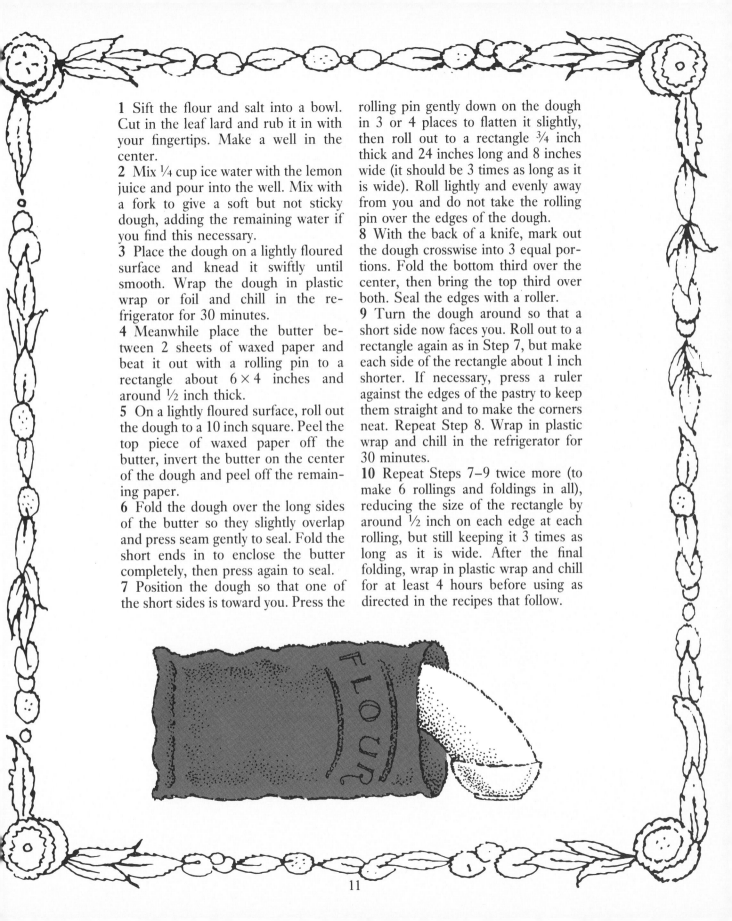

Top Crust Pies

Savory mixtures of meat, fish and vegetables are topped with melt-in-the-mouth crumbly, puff or cheese pastry. Whether you choose an economical pie such as spicy sausage or something more exotic, like Beef and mushroom, with its wine, olive and anchovy sauce these satisfying top crust pies will make memorable main meals for you and your family. Only the most wholesome ingredients are used in these pies straight from the country kitchen.

Steak & parsnip pie

Serves 4

2 tablespoons vegetable oil
1½ lb chuck steak, cut in bite-size pieces
1 large onion, sliced
¼ cup all-purpose flour
1 can (16 oz) tomatoes
2 chicken bouillon cubes
bouquet garni
salt and freshly ground black pepper
1½ cups parsnips cut in chunky pieces
½ lb Puff pastry (see page 10)
a little beaten egg, for glaze

1 Preheat the oven to 350°F.
2 Heat the oil in a Dutch oven, add the meat and onion and cook until the onion is soft and the meat is browned on all sides. Sprinkle in the flour, then cook for 1–2 minutes, stirring the mixture constantly.
3 Stir in the tomatoes and their juice, crumble in the bouillon cubes and stir well to mix. Add the bouquet garni and season to taste with salt and pepper. Bring to a boil, stirring, then cover and transfer to the oven. Cook for 1½ hours or until the meat is just tender.
4 Stir in the parsnips and cook for 45 minutes more.
5 Meanwhile, roll out the pastry on a floured surface to a shape slightly larger than the circumference of a 1½ quart pie dish. Cut off a long narrow strip of pastry all around the edge.

Reserve this and other trimmings.
6 Transfer the meat and parsnip mixture to the pie dish, then discard the bouquet garni and taste and adjust seasoning. Increase the oven temperature to 425°F. Brush the rim of the pie dish with water, then press the narrow strip of pastry all around the rim. Brush the strip with a little more water, then place the large piece of pastry on top. Trim the edge of the pastry, then seal and crimp.
7 Make leaves or other shapes with the trimmings, then brush the undersides with water and fix firmly to the piecrust. Make a small steam slit in the center then brush all over the crust with beaten egg.
8 Bake the pie in the oven for 25–30 minutes until the crust is well risen and golden brown. Serve hot.

Beef & mushroom pie

Serves 4

2 tablespoons all-purpose flour
salt and freshly ground black pepper
1½ lb rump steak or chuck steak, cut in ¾ inch cubes
¾ lb Puff pastry (see page 10)
¾ cup butter
1 large onion, finely sliced
6 large flat mushrooms, stems removed and reserved
1¼ cups beef stock
½ cup red wine
bouquet garni
3 anchovy fillets, pounded
2 tablespoons Dijon mustard
1 tablespoon Worcestershire sauce
¾ cup stuffed olives
TO FINISH
1 egg, beaten, for glaze

1 Preheat the oven to 325°F. Put the flour in a plastic bag and season with salt and pepper. Add the beef cubes and shake to coat them thoroughly. Shake off any excess flour.

2 Roll out the pastry on a lightly floured surface to a shape about 1½ inches larger than the circumference of a 1½ quart deep pie dish. Cut off a long narrow strip all around the edge. Reserve with the other trimmings.

3 Melt half the butter in a Dutch oven, add the onion and sauté for 5 minutes. Add the beef cubes and brown on all sides over high heat.

4 Lower the heat slightly and stir in the mushroom stems, stock, wine, bouquet garni, anchovy fillets, mustard and Worcestershire. Add the olives and bring the liquid to the simmering point, stirring all the time.

5 Cover the pot and cook in the oven for 1½–2 hours, until the meat is just tender, then remove from the oven. If there is a lot of liquid left, strain it off into a pan and reduce by rapid boiling to about ¾ cup. Return to the pot and let cool.

6 Raise the oven temperature to 425°F. Melt the remaining butter in a very large skillet, then sauté the mushroom caps, in batches if necessary, for about 2 minutes each side. Set aside.

7 Arrange the ingredients in layers in the pie dish, starting with mushroom caps, then a layer of meat and so on, finishing with a meat layer.

8 Brush the rim of the pie dish with water, then press the narrow strip of pastry all around the rim. Brush the strip with a little more water, then place the large piece of pastry on top.

Trim the edge of the pastry and crimp.

9 Glaze the top of the pie with the beaten egg and make a steam slit. Bake in the oven for 15 minutes, then lower the temperature to 350°F and cook for 30 minutes more. Serve hot.

Bacon & apple pie

Serves 4

½ lb Basic pie dough (see page 10)
12 bacon slices, chopped
1 large onion, thinly sliced
2 medium-size potatoes, cut in ⅛ inch slices
2 tart apples
freshly ground black pepper
1 cup hard cider
butter, for greasing
milk, for glaze

1 Preheat the oven to 400°F. Grease a 1½ quart pie dish.

2 Roll out the dough on a floured surface to a shape slightly larger than the circumference of the pie dish. Cut off a long narrow strip of dough all around the edge. Reserve this and other trimmings.

3 Put the bacon, onion and potatoes in a bowl. Pare, core and slice the apples, then add to the bowl with plenty of pepper. Stir well to mix. Transfer the mixture to the greased pie dish, then pour over the cider.

4 Brush the rim of the pie dish with water, then press the narrow strip of pastry all around the rim. Brush the strip with a little more water, then place the large piece of dough on top. Trim the edge of the dough then seal and crimp.

5 Make leaves or other shapes with the dough trimmings, then brush the undersides with water and fix them firmly on the piecrust. Make a small steam slit in the center of the crust, then brush all over the crust with milk.

6 Bake in the oven for 20 minutes, then lower the temperature to 350°F and bake for 30–40 minutes more until the potatoes are tender when pierced with a fine skewer. Serve hot.

Spicy sausage pie

Serves 4

3 tablespoons butter
1 lb spiced pork sausage links, cut in 1 inch slices
2 hard-cooked eggs, quartered
salt and freshly ground black pepper
1 onion, chopped
1 small green pepper, seeded and chopped
1 clove garlic, minced (optional)
¼ teaspoon chili powder
2 teaspoons all-purpose flour
1 can (8 oz) tomatoes
1 teaspoon chopped fresh sage, or ½ teaspoon dried sage
½ lb Basic pie dough (see page 10)
milk, for glaze

1 Preheat the oven to 375°F.

2 Melt 1 tablespoon butter in a large skillet, add the sausage slices and cook quickly over brisk heat, stirring, until browned on all sides. Remove from the skillet, drain on kitchen paper towels and arrange in a round 9 inch ovenproof pie plate with the quartered hard-cooked eggs. Season with salt and freshly ground black pepper.

3 Melt the remaining butter in a saucepan, add the onion, green pepper and garlic, if using, and sauté gently for 5 minutes until softened. Sprinkle in the chili powder and flour, sauté for 1 minute more, stirring, then add the canned tomatoes with their juice. Stir well and bring to the simmering point, then add the sage and salt and pepper to taste. Simmer, uncovered, for 5 minutes. Let cool, then pour the mixture over the sausage slices and eggs.

4 Roll out the dough on a lightly floured board to a round slightly larger than the pie plate. Cut off a strip all around the edge. Reserve the trimmings. Brush the rim of the plate with water, then press the strip all around the rim. Brush the strip with a little more water and cover with the top crust. Seal, and crimp.

5 Make leaves and other decors from the dough trimmings, brush the undersides with milk and press onto the pie-crust lid. Make a small slit in the center and brush all over with milk.

6 Bake the pie in the oven for 30 minutes until the top crust is golden brown. Serve the pie hot, cut in wedges.

Homestead pie

Serves 4–6

1 lb tart apples
juice of ½ lemon
¾ lb Puff pastry (see page 10)
2 lb lean pork, cut in 1 inch cubes
salt and freshly ground black pepper
1 tablespoon fresh sage or 1½ teaspoons dried sage
1 tablespoon sugar
1¼ cups hard cider
1 egg, beaten, for glaze

1 Preheat the oven to 425°F.

2 Pare, core and slice the apples into water acidulated with the lemon juice.

3 Roll out the pastry on a lightly floured surface to a shape slightly larger than the circumference of a 1½ quart pie dish. Cut off a long narrow strip all around the edge. Reserve with other trimmings.

4 Arrange half the pork in the bottom of the pie dish. Season with salt and freshly ground black pepper and half the sage. Drain the apple slices and place them in a layer over the meat.

5 Sprinkle the apples with sugar, then top with the remaining pork. Season with salt, pepper and the remaining sage. Pour in the cider.

6 Brush the rim of the pie dish with water, then press the narrow strip of pastry all around the rim. Brush the strip with a little more water, then place the large piece of pastry on top. Trim the edge of the pastry, then seal and crimp.

7 Make pastry leaves with the rolled out trimmings. Brush the undersides with beaten egg and fix firmly to the piecrust. Glaze the piecrust with beaten egg and make a steam slit in the center.

8 Bake in the oven for 15 minutes, then reduce temperature to 350°F and bake for 1¼ hours more. If the crust starts to brown, cover it with foil. Serve hot.

Lamb & cider pie

Serves 4

3 tablespoons shortening
12 arm or blade lamb chops, trimmed of excess fat
1 teaspoon dried rosemary
salt and freshly ground black pepper
2 large Bermuda onions, thinly sliced
1 tablespoon all-purpose flour
2 cups hard cider or chicken stock
2 large tart apples, pared, cored and sliced
½ lb Basic pie dough (see page 10)
milk, for glaze

1 Preheat the oven to 400°F.

2 Melt the shortening in a large skillet, add the chops and cook for 2 minutes on each side. Remove with a slotted spoon and arrange in a rectangular pie dish. Sprinkle over the herbs and season with salt and pepper.

3 Add the onions to the fat remaining in the skillet and sauté gently for 5 minutes, until they are soft and lightly colored. Sprinkle over the flour and cook for 2 minutes, stirring constantly.

4 Add the cider gradually to the pan, stirring constantly with a wooden spoon. Bring to a boil, lower the heat and simmer without stirring for 2 minutes.

5 Cover the chops with apple slices, then spoon the onion mixture on top.

6 Roll out the dough on a floured surface to a shape slightly larger than the top of the pie dish. Cut off 4 narrow strips all around the edge and reserve all the trimmings. Brush the rim of the dish with water and press the strips of dough onto the rim. Brush the strips with a little more water, then place the larger piece of dough on top. Trim the edges, seal and crimp.

7 Make leaves with the dough trimmings, brush the undersides with water and press onto the piecrust. Make a small steam slit in the center of the pie, then brush with milk.

8 Put the pie dish on a baking sheet and cook in the oven for 15 minutes. Lower the heat to 350°F and cook for 30 minutes more, covering the crust with wet waxed paper if it starts to brown too quickly. Serve hot.

Corn pie

Serves 4

3 tablespoons butter
1 onion, chopped
1 small green pepper, seeded and diced
¼ cup all-purpose flour
1¼ cups milk
½ teaspoon dried mixed herbs
1½ packages (10 oz size) frozen whole kernel corn
1 cup diced cooked ham
salt and freshly ground black pepper
beaten egg, for glaze
CHEESE PASTRY
1½ cups all-purpose flour
pinch of salt
⅓ cup butter
¾ cup shredded sharp Cheddar cheese
⅓ cup ice water

1 Make the filling: Melt the butter in a saucepan, add the onion and sauté for 5 minutes until soft.

2 Add the green pepper to the pan and continue to sauté for 2 minutes.

3 Sprinkle in the flour, then stir over low heat for 1–2 minutes. Off heat, gradually stir in the milk, then return to the heat and simmer, stirring, until thick and smooth.

4 Add the herbs, frozen corn and ham and simmer for 3 minutes. Season to taste with salt and pepper, then cool.

5 Meanwhile, make the pastry: Sift the flour and a pinch of salt into a bowl. Cut in the butter and rub it in with your fingertips until the mixture resembles coarse meal. Stir in the cheese, then sprinkle in the water and draw the mixture together to a firm dough. Wrap the dough in plastic wrap and refrigerate for 30 minutes.

6 Preheat the oven to 400°F.

7 Roll out the pastry on a lightly floured surface to a shape slightly larger than the top of a 1 quart pie dish. Cut off a narrow strip of pastry from the edge and reserve.

8 Transfer the corn mixture to the pie dish, mounding the corn in the center. Brush the rim of the pie dish with water, then press the strip of pastry onto the rim. Brush the strip with water, then place the large piece of pastry on top. Trim the edge, then seal and crimp. Use the trimmings to decorate the pie: Brush the undersides with water and fix on the top crust.

9 Brush the pie with beaten egg, make a steam slit in the center and bake in the oven for about 30 minutes until the top crust is crisp and golden brown.

Eastern chicken pie

Serves 4–6

¼ cup butter
1 onion, chopped
2 tablespoons seedless raisins
2 teaspoons curry powder
¼ cup all-purpose flour
1¼ cups chicken stock
2 teaspoons lemon juice
3 cups cooked chicken chunks
1 cup sliced mushrooms
salt and freshly ground black pepper
3 tomatoes, peeled and roughly chopped
½ lb Puff pastry (see page 10)
beaten egg, for glaze

1 Preheat the oven to 425°F.
2 Melt the butter in a large skillet, add the onion and sauté for 5 minutes until soft and lightly colored. Add the raisins and curry powder and cook gently for another 5 minutes. Sprinkle in the flour and stir until blended. Gradually stir in the stock and lemon juice and simmer, stirring, until thick and smooth.
3 Stir in the chicken chunks and mushrooms and season with salt and pepper to taste. Cook for 5 minutes more, then stir in the chopped tomatoes. Pour the mixture into a 1 quart pie dish.
4 Roll out the pastry on a floured surface to a shape slightly larger than the top of the pie dish. Cut off a strip of pastry all around the edge.
5 Brush the rim of the dish with water and press the strip of pastry on the rim. Brush the strip with a little more water, then place the large piece of pastry on top. Press to seal, then crimp the edge.
6 Make decors with the pastry trimmings, brush the undersides with water and fix them firmly to the pie-crust. Brush the crust all over with the beaten egg and make a small steam slit in the center of the pie. Bake in the oven for 30 minutes until golden. Serve at once.

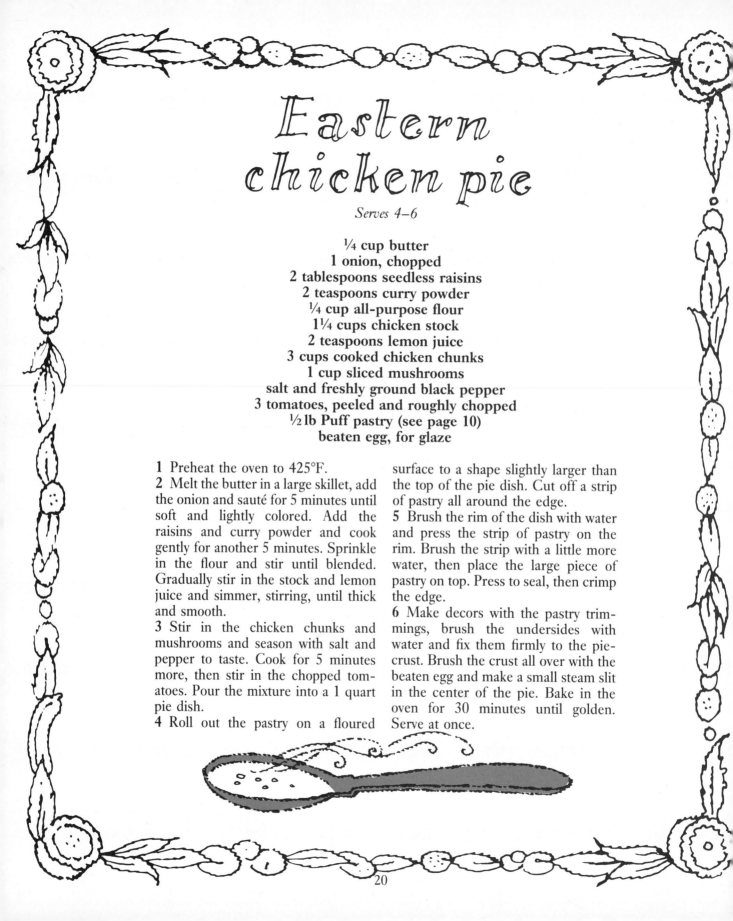

Farmhouse turkey & ham pie

Serves 4

¾ lb Puff pastry (see page 10)
2 cups chopped cooked turkey
2 cups chopped cooked ham
2 hard-cooked eggs, quartered
a little beaten egg, for glaze
SAUCE
2 tablespoons butter
¼ cup all-purpose flour
1¼ cups milk
finely grated rind and juice of ½ lemon
1 tablespoon minced fresh parsley
salt and freshly ground black pepper

1 Preheat the oven to 425°F.

2 Roll out the pastry on a lightly floured surface to a shape slightly larger than the circumference of a 1 quart pie dish. Cut off a long narrow strip all around the edge. Reserve with other trimmings.

3 Mix the turkey and ham together in the pie dish and arrange the quartered eggs on top.

4 Make the sauce: Melt the butter in a small saucepan, sprinkle in the flour and stir over low heat for 1–2 minutes until straw-colored. Off heat, gradually stir in the milk. Return to the heat and simmer, stirring, until the sauce is thick and smooth.

5 Remove from the heat and stir in the lemon rind and juice, and the parsley. Season to taste with salt and pepper and let cool. Pour evenly over the turkey and ham in the pie dish.

6 Brush the rim of the pie dish with water, and then press the narrow strip of pastry all around the rim. Brush the strip with a little more water, then place the large piece of pastry on top. Trim the edge of the pastry, then seal and crimp.

7 Make leaves with the pastry trimmings, brush the undersides with water and fix firmly to the piecrust. Brush with beaten egg and make a small steam slit in the center of the piecrust.

8 Bake in the oven for 25–30 minutes until the crust is well risen and golden brown. Serve hot or cold.

Mariners pie

Serves 4

½ lb Puff pastry (see page 10)
lightly beaten egg white, for glaze
lemon wedges, for garnish
FILLING
3 tablespoons butter
1 small onion, chopped
¼ cup all-purpose flour
1 cup milk
¼ cup dry white wine
1 can (16 oz) mussels in brine, drained
½ cup shelled shrimp, thawed if frozen
salt and freshly ground black pepper
1 tablespoon chopped fresh parsley

1 Roll out the pastry on a lightly floured board to a round 1½ inches larger than the top of a 1 quart pie dish. Cut off a strip all around the edge of the pastry. Reserve this and other trimmings.

2 Make the filling: Melt the butter in a heavy-bottomed saucepan, add the onion and sauté gently for about 5 minutes until it is soft and lightly colored. Sprinkle in the flour and stir over low heat for 1–2 minutes. Off heat, gradually stir in milk. Return to heat and simmer, stirring, until thick.

3 Stir in the wine, mussels and shrimp and season to taste with salt and pepper. Simmer for 2 minutes, then stir in the parsley. Pour the mixture into the dish and let stand until cold.

4 Preheat the oven to 425°F. Brush the rim of the pie dish with water, then press the narrow piece of pastry all around the rim. Brush the strip with a little more water, then place the larger piece of pastry on top. Trim the edge of the pastry, then seal and crimp. Make pie decors from the pastry trimmings and fix these firmly onto the piecrust with the egg white. Lightly brush the entire lid with egg white.

5 Bake in the oven for 20 minutes, then lower oven temperature to 375°F and bake for 15 minutes more until the pastry is puffed up and golden. Serve cut in portions and garnished with lemon wedges.

Saucy spinach & egg pie

Serves 4–6

¼ cup butter
½ cup all-purpose flour
1 teaspoon dry mustard
2½ cups milk
¾ cup shredded sharp Cheddar cheese
salt and freshly ground black pepper
3 hard-cooked eggs, sliced
1 cup sliced mushrooms
2 packages (10 oz size) leaf spinach, cooked and well drained
½ lb Puff pastry (see page 10)
2 tablespoons half-and-half, for glaze

1 Preheat the oven to 400°F.

2 Melt the butter in a small heavy-bottomed saucepan. Stir in the flour and dry mustard and cook over low heat for 1–2 minutes. Off heat, gradually stir in the milk. Return to heat and simmer, stirring, until thick and smooth. Stir in ½ cup shredded Cheddar and salt and pepper to taste.

3 Arrange half of the eggs over the base of a 10 inch shallow pie dish or pan, then top with a layer each of half the mushrooms and half the spinach. Pour over half the sauce. Repeat the layers with the remaining eggs, mushrooms, spinach and sauce and sprinkle the remaining shredded cheese over the top layer.

4 On a lightly floured surface, roll out the pastry and use to make a lid. Reserve the pastry trimmings.

5 Place pastry lid on top, pressing down the edges well to seal. Crimp the edge. Roll cut pastry trimmings and make decors. Fix to piecrust with a little of the half-and-half then brush the entire crust with half-and-half. Make a steam slit in the center of the piecrust.

6 Cook in the oven for 35–45 minutes, until the pie is golden brown. Serve at once, while piping hot.

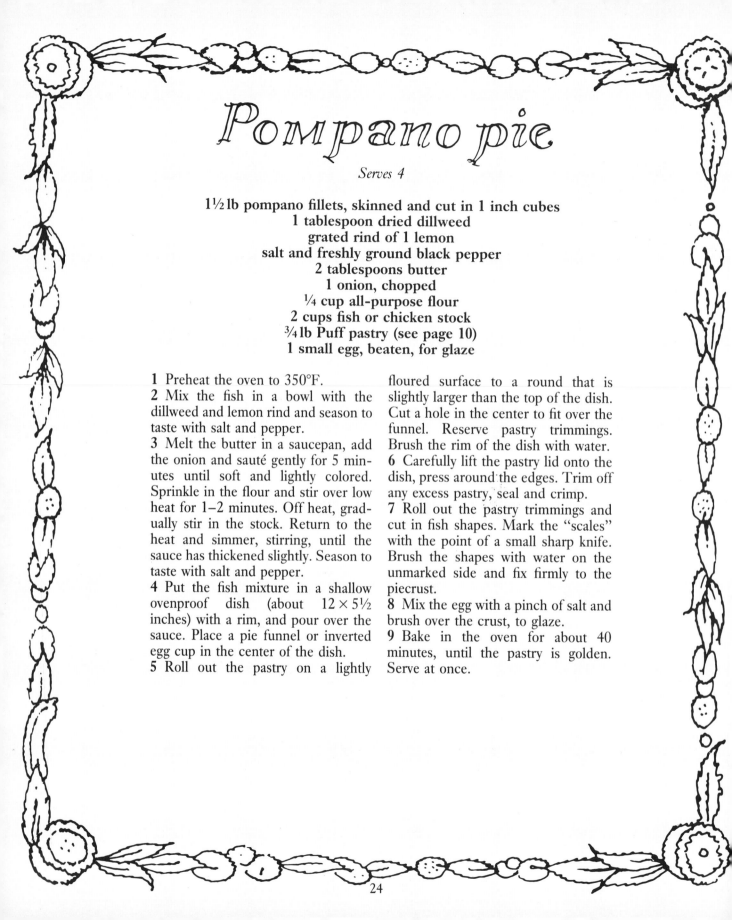

Pompano pie

Serves 4

1½ lb pompano fillets, skinned and cut in 1 inch cubes
1 tablespoon dried dillweed
grated rind of 1 lemon
salt and freshly ground black pepper
2 tablespoons butter
1 onion, chopped
¼ cup all-purpose flour
2 cups fish or chicken stock
¾ lb Puff pastry (see page 10)
1 small egg, beaten, for glaze

1 Preheat the oven to 350°F.

2 Mix the fish in a bowl with the dillweed and lemon rind and season to taste with salt and pepper.

3 Melt the butter in a saucepan, add the onion and sauté gently for 5 minutes until soft and lightly colored. Sprinkle in the flour and stir over low heat for 1–2 minutes. Off heat, gradually stir in the stock. Return to the heat and simmer, stirring, until the sauce has thickened slightly. Season to taste with salt and pepper.

4 Put the fish mixture in a shallow ovenproof dish (about 12 × 5½ inches) with a rim, and pour over the sauce. Place a pie funnel or inverted egg cup in the center of the dish.

5 Roll out the pastry on a lightly floured surface to a round that is slightly larger than the top of the dish. Cut a hole in the center to fit over the funnel. Reserve pastry trimmings. Brush the rim of the dish with water.

6 Carefully lift the pastry lid onto the dish, press around the edges. Trim off any excess pastry, seal and crimp.

7 Roll out the pastry trimmings and cut in fish shapes. Mark the "scales" with the point of a small sharp knife. Brush the shapes with water on the unmarked side and fix firmly to the piecrust.

8 Mix the egg with a pinch of salt and brush over the crust, to glaze.

9 Bake in the oven for about 40 minutes, until the pastry is golden. Serve at once.

Country pie

Serves 4–6

Cheese pastry (see page 19)
1 egg, beaten, for glaze
FILLING
2½ cups diced potatoes
3 carrots, sliced
⅔ cup frozen fava beans
3 leeks, cut in ½ inch slices
1 tablespoon chopped fresh parsley
salt and freshly ground black pepper
2 tablespoons butter
¼ cup all-purpose flour
1¼ cups vegetable or chicken stock

1 Preheat the oven to 375°F. Make the filling: Cook the potatoes, carrots and beans in boiling salted water for 10 minutes. Drain thoroughly, then place in a 1 quart pie dish with the leeks, mixing them well together. Sprinkle with the parsley and salt and pepper to taste. Set aside.

2 Melt the butter in a clean saucepan, sprinkle in the flour and stir over low heat for 1–2 minutes until straw-colored. Gradually stir in the stock, then bring to a boil. Reduce heat and simmer, stirring, until thick and smooth. Pour over the vegetables.

3 Roll out the cheese pastry on a floured surface to a shape slightly larger than the top of the pie dish. Cut off a long strip of pastry all around the edge. Reserve this and other trimmings. Brush the rim of the pie dish with water, then press the narrow strip of pastry all around the rim. Brush the strip with a little more water, then place the large piece of pastry on top. Press to seal, then trim. Crimp the edge of the pie.

4 Make decors from the trimmings, brush the undersides with water and fix to the crust with a little of the beaten egg. Brush the crust with the remaining beaten egg, and make a steam slit in the center. Bake in the oven for 35–40 minutes until the crust is golden brown and the vegetables are tender. Serve at once.

Open~Faced Pies

For sunny days and parties, on porch or patio, open-faced pies and quiches contain an array of mouthwatering fillings – curried shrimp, chicken and walnut, spinach and bacon and melt-in-the-mouth Brie are just a few. All of these pies can be made in advance and frozen until they are needed – ideal for when you are preparing food for a party, or for those occasions when friends drop by unexpectedly. Most of these quiches and pies can be served hot or cold; in the summer all that is needed to accompany them is a crunchy salad. Attractive and appetizing, these simple pies are sure to be popular!

Egg & vegetable pie

Serves 4

½ lb Basic pie dough (see page 10)
FILLING
3 tablespoons butter
1 cup sliced button mushrooms
¼ cup all-purpose flour
½ teaspoon curry powder
1¼ cups milk
4 hard-cooked eggs, neatly chopped
⅔ cup frozen peas, cooked
salt and freshly ground black pepper

1 Preheat the oven to 400°F.
2 Roll out the dough on a lightly floured surface and use it to line an 8 inch pie pan. Trim the edges and prick the base in several places with a fork. Place a round of waxed paper or foil in the pie shell and weight it down with a thick even layer of pie weights. Bake unfilled for 10 minutes.
3 Remove the waxed paper and weights, then return the pie shell to the oven. Bake for 10–15 minutes more, or until the shell is crisp and lightly golden.
4 Meanwhile, make the filling: Melt the butter in a saucepan and cook the mushrooms for 2–3 minutes, stirring occasionally. Remove from the pan with a slotted spoon, draining all the butter back into the pan.
5 Sprinkle the flour and curry powder into pan. Stir over low heat for 1–2 minutes. Off heat, gradually stir in the milk. Return to the heat and simmer, stirring, until thick and smooth.
6 Gently fold the chopped eggs and peas into the sauce. Season to taste with salt and pepper, then return to very low heat and warm through gently. Lastly, fold in the mushrooms. Pour the mixture into the cooked pie shell. Serve hot or cold.

Squash & pecan pie

Serves 4

½ lb Basic pie dough (see page 10)
¼ cup ground pecans
2 tablespoons butter
5 cups roughly chopped peeled acorn squash
1 large onion, chopped
salt and freshly ground black pepper
½ cup shredded Cheddar cheese
pecan halves and tomato slices, for garnish

1 Preheat the oven to 400°F.

2 Roll out the dough on a lightly floured surface and line a 9 inch fluted pie pan. Sprinkle half the pecans over the base of the pie shell and press lightly into the dough.

3 Prick the base with a fork. Place a large round of waxed paper or foil in the pie shell, weight it down with pie weights and bake unfilled in the oven for 15 minutes.

4 Meanwhile, melt the butter in a large skillet, add the squash and chopped onion, cover and cook gently for 20–25 minutes until the vegetables are soft. Season to taste with salt and black pepper and keep warm.

5 Remove the weights and waxed paper or foil from the pie shell and return to the oven for 10–15 minutes more, until the shell is crisp and the side is beginning to brown. The base of the pie shell must be quite dry at this stage or the cooked pie will be soggy and unappetizing.

6 Spoon the vegetables into the cooked pie shell and sprinkle the remaining ground pecans and the cheese on top. Return to the oven for 5 minutes until the cheese has melted.

7 Remove the pie from the oven and let cool for 5 minutes. Garnish with pecan halves and tomato slices and serve warm.

Mediterranean pie

Serves 4–6

½ lb Basic pie dough (see page 10)
FILLING
2 tablespoons butter
2 onions, minced
1 clove garlic, minced
½ teaspoon dried mixed herbs
salt and freshly ground black pepper
egg white, to seal (optional)
1 tablespoon Dijon mustard
4 medium-size tomatoes, peeled and thickly sliced
or 1 can (16 oz) tomatoes, drained
½ cup shredded Gruyère or Cheddar cheese
TOPPING
1 can (2 oz) anchovies in olive oil, drained
5 ripe olives, halved and pitted

1 Preheat the oven to 400°F.

2 Roll out the dough on a floured board and use to line an 8 inch springform pie pan. Prick the pie shell all over with a fork. Line the pie shell with waxed paper or foil and weight it down with pie weights or rice. Bake unfilled in the oven for 10 minutes.

3 Meanwhile, make the filling: Melt the butter in a skillet, add the onions and garlic and sauté gently for 10 minutes until golden brown. Sprinkle over the dried mixed herbs and season with salt and pepper.

4 Remove the waxed paper or foil lining and the weights from the pie shell, and brush the inside of the shell with beaten egg white, if liked. Return the pie shell to the oven and bake for 5 minutes more. Remove the pie shell from the oven and turn the temperature down to 350°F.

5 Spread the mustard over the baked pie shell, then cover it with the onion mixture and then a layer of overlapping slices of tomato. Sprinkle over the shredded cheese.

6 Arrange a lattice of anchovy fillets over the top of the cheese. Place half an olive, cut side down, in each diamond shape of the lattice.

7 Bake for about 30 minutes or until the crust is crisp and golden brown.

8 Before serving, let stand for 5–10 minutes then remove from the pan and place on a serving platter. Serve warm.

Red summer pie

Serves 4

Cheese pastry (see page 19)
lightly beaten egg white, to seal
FILLING
2 tablespoons vegetable oil
2 large sweet red peppers, seeded and thinly sliced
4 cloves garlic, minced
½ cup soft white bread crumbs
½ teaspoon dried basil
salt and freshly ground black pepper
3 large tomatoes, thinly sliced
1 teaspoon sugar

1 Preheat the oven to 400°F.

2 Roll out the pastry on a lightly floured surface and use to line a 9 inch springform pie pan. Prick the pastry with a fork. Place a large round of waxed paper or foil in the pie shell and weight it down with pie weights. Bake unfilled for 10 minutes.

3 Remove the paper or foil lining and weights, brush the inside of the pie shell with beaten egg white, then return the shell to the oven for 5 minutes more. Remove from the oven and set aside.

4 Make the filling: Heat the oil in a skillet, add the peppers and sauté gently for 5 minutes until beginning to soften. Add the garlic and continue to cook until soft and lightly colored. Set the filling aside.

5 Put the bread crumbs in a bowl with the basil and salt and pepper to taste. Mix well.

6 Spread the peppers over the base of the pie shell, then cover with the tomato slices. Sprinkle with sugar, then finish with a layer of the bread crumb mix.

7 Bake in the oven for 30–35 minutes until the tomatoes are tender and the pie shell is golden.

8 Serve the pie hot or cold.

Springtime pie

Serves 4

½ lb **Basic pie dough**
FILLING
1 cup cottage cheese with chives
3 eggs
2 tablespoons butter
1 cup sliced button mushrooms
½ teaspoon dried thyme
salt and freshly ground black pepper
1 tomato, thinly sliced

1 Preheat the oven to 400°F.

2 Roll out the pastry on a lightly floured surface and use to line an 8 inch springform pie pan. Prick the pastry with a fork, line with waxed paper and fill with pie weights Bake unfilled in the oven for 10 minutes.

3 Meanwhile, make the filling: Put the cottage cheese into a bowl with the chives and eggs and beat together with a fork until well mixed.

4 Melt the butter in a small saucepan, add the mushrooms and sauté gently for 2 minutes, stirring. Drain well, then add the mushrooms to the cottage cheese mixture. Stir in the thyme and season to taste with salt and pepper.

5 Remove the waxed paper and weights from the pie shell, pour in the cottage cheese mixture and arrange the tomato slices around the edge. Return to the oven and bake for 35 minutes until the filling is golden brown and set.

6 Let the pie stand for 5–10 minutes. Remove the pan and place thepie on a serving platter. Serve while still warm or leave until cold.

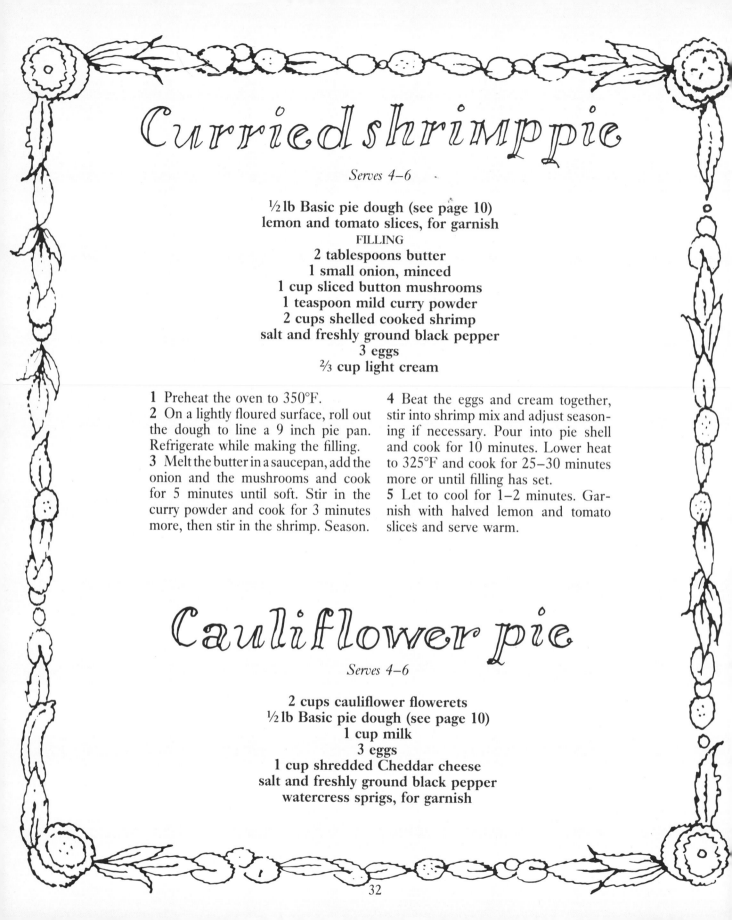

Curried shrimp pie

Serves 4–6

½ lb Basic pie dough (see page 10)
lemon and tomato slices, for garnish
FILLING
2 tablespoons butter
1 small onion, minced
1 cup sliced button mushrooms
1 teaspoon mild curry powder
2 cups shelled cooked shrimp
salt and freshly ground black pepper
3 eggs
⅔ cup light cream

1 Preheat the oven to 350°F.
2 On a lightly floured surface, roll out the dough to line a 9 inch pie pan. Refrigerate while making the filling.
3 Melt the butter in a saucepan, add the onion and the mushrooms and cook for 5 minutes until soft. Stir in the curry powder and cook for 3 minutes more, then stir in the shrimp. Season.

4 Beat the eggs and cream together, stir into shrimp mix and adjust seasoning if necessary. Pour into pie shell and cook for 10 minutes. Lower heat to 325°F and cook for 25–30 minutes more or until filling has set.
5 Let to cool for 1–2 minutes. Garnish with halved lemon and tomato slices and serve warm.

Cauliflower pie

Serves 4–6

2 cups cauliflower flowerets
½ lb Basic pie dough (see page 10)
1 cup milk
3 eggs
1 cup shredded Cheddar cheese
salt and freshly ground black pepper
watercress sprigs, for garnish

1 Preheat the oven to 400°F.
2 Place cauliflower in a large saucepan and just cover with cold water. Bring to a boil and boil for about 5 minutes. Drain, rinse well under cold water, then drain again very thoroughly and pat quite dry.
3 On a lightly floured surface, roll out the dough to line an 8 inch springform pie pan.
4 Arrange the cauliflower flowerets, stems down, in the pie shell. In a bowl, beat together the milk, eggs and ¾ cup of the cheese, season to taste with salt and pepper and pour over cauliflower. Sprinkle evenly with the remaining shredded Cheddar cheese.
5 Cook in the oven for 30–40 minutes until the filling has only just set. Remove from the oven, let cool slightly, then carefully remove from the pie pan and slide onto a serving platter. Serve at once, garnished with sprigs of watercress.

Salami quiche

Serves 4

½ lb Basic pie dough (see page 10)
lightly beaten egg white to seal
FILLING
2 eggs, lightly beaten
¾ cup cottage cheese
1 cup chopped Italian salami
2 tablespoons capers, rinsed and chopped
salt and freshly ground black pepper

1 Preheat the oven to 400°F.
2 Roll out the dough on a lightly floured surface and use to line an 8 inch springform pie pan. Prick the dough all over with a fork, then line the pie shell with foil or waxed paper and weight down with pie weights. Bake unfilled in the oven for 30 minutes.
3 Remove the weights and foil, then brush the inside of the pie shell with beaten egg white. Return to the oven for 5 minutes more. Remove from the oven and lower the temperature to 350°F.
4 Mix the beaten eggs with the cottage cheese, salami and capers. Season with a little salt and pepper.
5 Spoon the filling into the pie shell, return to the oven and bake for 25–30 minutes more until set.
6 To serve: Remove the quiche from the pan and transfer to a serving platter. Serve warm or cold.

Carrot & nut pie

Serves 4–6

2½ cups thinly sliced carrots
½ lb Basic pie dough (see page 10)
6 eggs
1 teaspoon hot Madras curry powder
1 teaspoon cumin seeds
1 cup pignoli or chopped walnuts

1 Preheat the oven to 400°F.
2 Steam the carrots for 20 minutes or until tender. Let them cool slightly.
3 On a lightly floured surface, roll out the dough to line a 9 inch pie pan.
4 Beat the eggs with the curry powder and cumin seeds. Arrange the carrot slices in overlapping rings in the pie shell. Scatter the nuts over the top and pour in the egg mixture, making sure the nuts are evenly distributed.
5 Bake the pie for about 25 minutes or until the filling is set and golden brown. Serve warm.

Spinach quiche

Serves 4–6

½ lb Basic pie dough (see page 10)
egg white, to seal (optional)
2 large eggs, beaten
1 package (10 oz) frozen chopped spinach, thawed and well drained
1 small onion, minced
⅔ cup light cream
2 bacon slices, chopped and cooked until crisp
½ cup shredded Cheddar cheese
¼ teaspoon freshly grated nutmeg
salt and freshly ground black pepper

1 Preheat the oven to 400°F.
2 Roll out the dough on a floured board and line an 8 inch springform pie pan. Prick the dough all over with a fork. Line the pie shell with waxed paper or foil and weight it down with pie weights or rice. Bake unfilled in the oven for 10 minutes.

3 Remove the waxed paper or foil lining and the beans or rice, and brush the inside of the pie shell with beaten egg white, if wished. Return the pie shell to the oven and bake for 5 minutes more. Remove from the oven and set aside. Turn the temperature down to 350°F.

4 Put the eggs, spinach, onion, cream, bacon and cheese in a large bowl and mix together thoroughly. Add the nutmeg and plenty of salt and pepper. Pour the mixture into the pie shell.

5 Bake the quiche in the oven for about 30 minutes until the filling is firm in the center.

6 Before serving, let stand for at least 5–10 minutes after removing from oven, then remove from pan and place on a serving platter.

Chicken quiche

Serves 4–6

½ lb Basic pie dough (see page 10)
lightly beaten egg white, to seal
watercress sprigs, for garnish
FILLING
2 cups minced cooked chicken
1 cup roughly chopped walnuts
½ cup finely shredded Gruyère cheese
large pinch of freshly grated nutmeg
salt and freshly ground black pepper
2 eggs
⅔ cup milk

1 Preheat the oven to 400°F

2 Roll out the dough on a floured surface and use it to line an 8 inch springform pie pan. Prick dough all over with a fork. Place a large round of waxed paper or foil in the pie shell and weight it down with pie weights.

3 Bake in the oven for 10 minutes. Remove the lining and weights, brush the inside of the pie shell with beaten egg white, then return to the oven for 5 minutes more.

4 Mix the chicken with the walnuts and half the cheese. Add nutmeg and season with salt and pepper.

5 Spread the mixture evenly in the prepared shell.

6 Beat eggs and milk together and pour over filling.

7 Sprinkle the remaining cheeseon top. Place in the oven and bake for about 30–35 minutes until set and golden on top.

8 Serve the quiche warm or cold, cut in wedges and garnished with the watercress sprigs.

Zucchini quiche

Serves 4–6

Cheese pastry (see page 19)
FILLING
2 tablespoons butter
2 cups shredded zucchini
3 eggs, beaten
⅓ cup light cream
⅓ cup milk
½–1 teaspoon oregano
salt and freshly ground black pepper

1 Roll out the pastry on a floured surface and use to line a 9 inch springform pie pan. Refrigerate for 30 minutes.

2 Preheat the oven to 400°F.

3 Remove the pie shell from the refrigerator, and prick the pastry in several places with a fork. Line the pie shell with waxed paper or foil and weight down with pie weights. Bake in the oven for 10 minutes.

4 Remove the pie shell from the oven. Lift out the waxed paper and weights. Brush the inside of the pie shell with a little of the beaten egg from the filling. Lower the oven temperature to 375°F and return the pie shell to the oven for 5 minutes more.

5 Meanwhile, melt 2 tablespoons butter in a skillet, add the zucchini and sauté over moderate heat for 3–5 minutes, stirring once or twice, until they begin to soften. Remove the pan from the heat.

6 In a bowl, beat the eggs, cream and milk together, with oregano to taste. Season well with salt and pepper.

7 Remove the pie shell from the oven and spoon the zucchini evenly over the base, then pour the egg mixture over the zucchini.

8 Bake the quiche in the oven for 15 minutes. Lower the temperature to 350°F and cook for 20 minutes more, until the filling is set and golden brown on top. Serve warm or cold.

Brie quiche

Serves 4

½ lb Basic pie dough (see page 10)
lightly beaten egg white, to seal
sliced tomato, for garnish
FILLING
½ lb Brie cheese, rind removed and cut in 1 inch squares
⅔ cup light cream
3 eggs
½ teaspoon light brown sugar
pinch of ground ginger
pinch of ground turmeric
pinch of salt

1 Preheat the oven to 400°F.

2 On a lightly floured surface, roll out the dough and line an 8 inch spring-form pie pan. Prick the dough lightly with a fork. Place a large round of waxed paper or foil in the pie shell and weight it down with pie weights. Bake in the oven for 10 minutes.

3 Remove the weights and paper or foil, brush the inside of the pie shell with beaten egg white, and return the shell to the oven for 5 minutes more.

4 Meanwhile, put the cheese (but not the rind) in a blender or food processor with the remaining filling ingredients and work until smooth.

5 Lower the oven temperature to 350°F. Arrange the squares of Brie rind over the base of the pie shell and pour over the filling. Bake in the oven for 30–40 minutes. The squares of rind will rise to the top of the filling to form a golden brown crust.

6 To serve: Let the quiche cool for about 15 minutes. Remove from the pan and transfer to a warm serving platter. Garnish with tomato, and serve warm or cold.

Double Crust Pies

All these pies have tasty fillings encased in pastry. Some are classic double crusts, with pastry top and bottom, others are made jelly-roll fashion and served in slices, while the rest are made by packaging the filling in a pastry 'wrapper'. Many vegetable variations are used to fill these appetizing double crust pies – there's a rich herbed potato mixture, a pie filled with Jerusalem artichokes and cheese, and a traditional Russian 'koulibiaka' – buttery puff pastry filled with cabbage and eggs. All the pies in this chapter are perfect for lunch and supper, and some can be served hot or cold.

Veal pie

Serves 4–5

1 lb Puff pastry (see page 10)
1 egg, beaten, for glaze
FOR THE FILLING
2 tablespoons butter
1 medium-size onion, chopped
½ lb pie veal, finely chopped
1 medium-size tart apple, pared, cored and chopped
2 tablespoons candied lemon peel, finely chopped
⅔ cup chicken stock
pinch of nutmeg
½ teaspoon freshly ground black pepper
1 tablespoon cornstarch

1 Make the filling: Melt the butter in a saucepan over low heat and sauté the onion until soft. Add the veal and stir over moderate heat until it changes color. Mix in the apple, lemon peel, stock, nutmeg, salt and pepper and bring to a boil. Cover, reduce the heat and simmer for 10 minutes.

2 Mix the cornstarch with a little cold water, add to the pan and bring back to a boil, stirring constantly. Reduce heat and simmer for 2 minutes. Remove from the heat.

3 Preheat the oven to 425°F. Roll out half the pastry thinly and use it to line a deep 8 inch pie dish. Roll out the remaining pastry and use it to form a lid for the pie.

4 Spoon the filling into the pie shell, brush the edges of the pastry with the beaten egg, put on the lid and seal well. Crimp the edges and cut a steam slit. Use the trimmings to make pastry leaves for decoration. Use some of the beaten egg to fix the decors onto the piecrust, then brush the entire crust with beaten egg.

5 Bake in the oven for 10 minutes, then reduce the heat to 375°F and continue cooking for 20–25 minutes more, or until well risen and golden brown. Serve hot or warm.

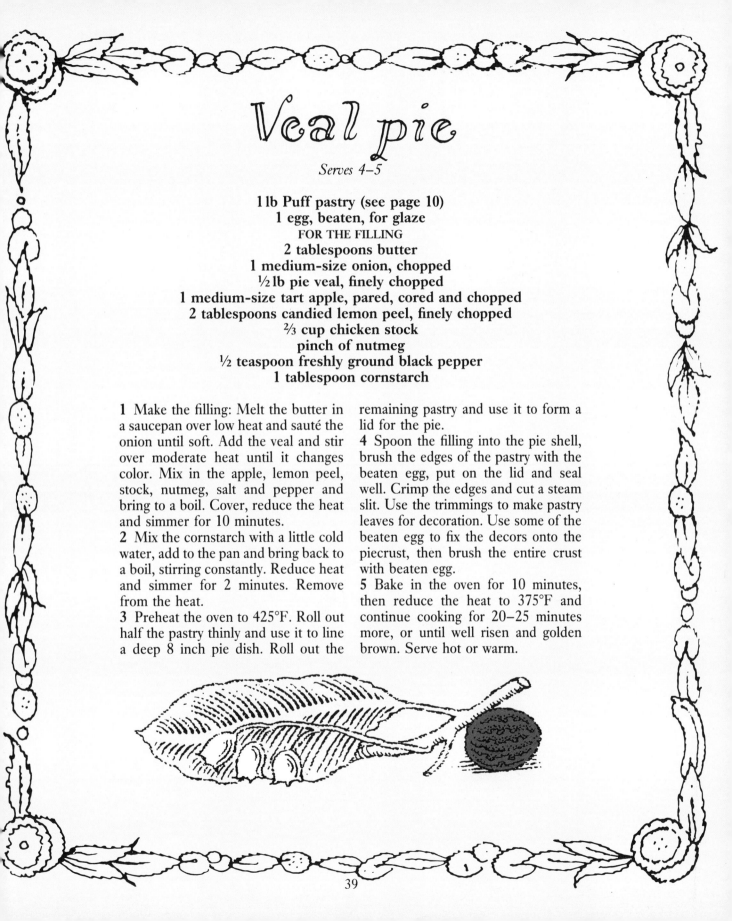

Chicken & chicken liver pie

Serves 4

¾ lb Basic pie dough (see page 10)
flour for dusting
¾ lb chicken parts
sprig of fresh thyme
2 bay leaves
12 black peppercorns
4 pearl onions
2 tablespoons dry white wine
¼ cup butter
½ lb chicken livers
3 large onions, minced
1 blade of mace
⅔ cup milk
½ teaspoon dried mixed herbs
salt and freshly ground black pepper
1 egg, beaten for glaze
3 tablespoons heavy cream

1 Cut off two-thirds of the dough and, on a lightly floured surface, roll out to a 12 inch round. Line an 8 inch pie plate with the dough.

2 Roll out the remaining one-third of the dough trimmings to make a top crust and use the trimmings to make decors. Chill all the dough in the refrigerator for 30 minutes.

3 Put the chicken in a large kettle and pour in enough water to cover. Add the thyme, bay leaves, peppercorns, onions and white wine and simmer gently for 30–40 minutes until the chicken is just cooked. Remove and reserve the chicken, strain the stock and set aside.

4 Melt the butter in a large skillet and sauté the chicken livers for 2 minutes, stirring occasionally. Remove with a slotted spoon and reserve.

5 Add the onions to the pan and sauté for 5 minutes until they begin to soften and color. Pour in the reserved stock, add the mace blade and the milk and bring to a boil. Lower the heat slightly and cook until the onions are very soft and the total quantity of onions and liquid is reduced to about 1½ cups. Take the pan off the heat, remove the mace blade and let cool.

6 Take the chicken flesh off the

bones, discard the skin and cut the flesh into large chunks. Roughly mash the chicken livers and mix them into the onion mix, then lightly fold in the chicken. Stir in the mixed herbs and season to taste.

7 Preheat the oven to 375°F. Pile the chicken mix into the pie shell, doming it slightly in the center.

8 Brush the edges of the dough with water and put on the crust, pressing the edges firmly together with your thumbs. Trim and crisp the edges of the pie. Make leaves from the pastry trimmings. Cut a steam slit in the piecrust; fix the trimmings firmly in place with a little of the beaten egg yolk. Use the remaining egg yolk to glaze the entire piecrust.

9 Cook for 1 hour until crust is cooked and golden. Add the cream through the steam slit 10 minutes before the end of the cooking time. Serve hot.

Bacon & egg pie

Serves 4

¾ lb Puff pastry (see page 10)
2 tablespoons vegetable oil
2 onions, finely chopped
12 bacon slices, diced
1½ cups finely diced potatoes
salt and freshly ground black pepper
4 eggs
1 egg, beaten, for glaze

1 Preheat the oven to 375°F.

2 Roll out just over half the pastry on a lightly floured surface and use to line an 8 inch pie pan. Roll out the remaining pastry to a round slightly larger than the pie pan, and set aside with the trimmings.

3 Heat the oil in a large skillet, add the onions and bacon and cook, stirring once or twice, for about 2–3 minutes. Add the potatoes, season with salt and pepper and cook for 5 minutes, stirring from time to time.

4 Spoon the mixture into the pie shell and spread it evenly over the base. Make 4 hollows in the mix and break an egg into each prepared hollow.

5 Brush the edge of the pastry with water and place the reserved pastry round on top. Trim the edge, and press lightly but firmly to seal.

6 Make leaves with the pastry trimmings, brush the undersides with beaten egg and fix to the pie crust. Make a steam slit in the center and brush all over with egg.

7 Bake the pie in the oven for 30–35 minutes until the pastry is well risen and golden brown. Serve hot or cold, cut in wedges.

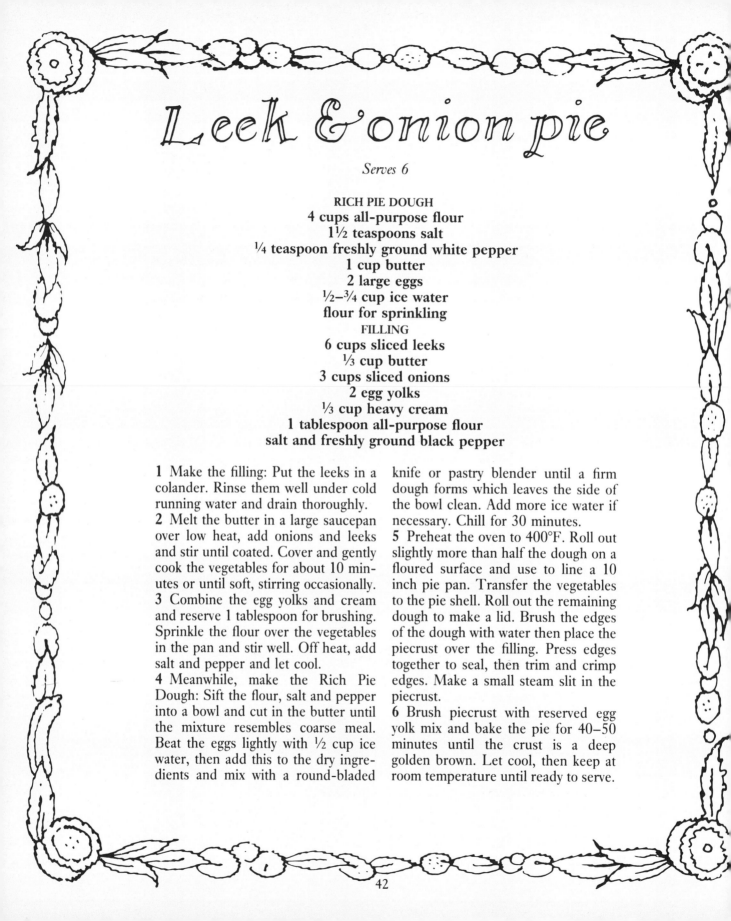

Leek & onion pie

Serves 6

RICH PIE DOUGH
4 cups all-purpose flour
1½ teaspoons salt
¼ teaspoon freshly ground white pepper
1 cup butter
2 large eggs
½–¾ cup ice water
flour for sprinkling
FILLING
6 cups sliced leeks
⅓ cup butter
3 cups sliced onions
2 egg yolks
⅓ cup heavy cream
1 tablespoon all-purpose flour
salt and freshly ground black pepper

1 Make the filling: Put the leeks in a colander. Rinse them well under cold running water and drain thoroughly.

2 Melt the butter in a large saucepan over low heat, add onions and leeks and stir until coated. Cover and gently cook the vegetables for about 10 minutes or until soft, stirring occasionally.

3 Combine the egg yolks and cream and reserve 1 tablespoon for brushing. Sprinkle the flour over the vegetables in the pan and stir well. Off heat, add salt and pepper and let cool.

4 Meanwhile, make the Rich Pie Dough: Sift the flour, salt and pepper into a bowl and cut in the butter until the mixture resembles coarse meal. Beat the eggs lightly with ½ cup ice water, then add this to the dry ingredients and mix with a round-bladed knife or pastry blender until a firm dough forms which leaves the side of the bowl clean. Add more ice water if necessary. Chill for 30 minutes.

5 Preheat the oven to 400°F. Roll out slightly more than half the dough on a floured surface and use to line a 10 inch pie pan. Transfer the vegetables to the pie shell. Roll out the remaining dough to make a lid. Brush the edges of the dough with water then place the piecrust over the filling. Press edges together to seal, then trim and crimp edges. Make a small steam slit in the piecrust.

6 Brush piecrust with reserved egg yolk mix and bake the pie for 40–50 minutes until the crust is a deep golden brown. Let cool, then keep at room temperature until ready to serve.

Herbed potato pie

Serves 6

Rich Pie Dough (see page 42)
1 egg yolk, beaten, for glaze
FILLING
2 lb medium-size waxy potatoes, thinly sliced
salt and freshly ground black pepper
4 tablespoons chopped fresh parsley
2 tablespoons chopped chervil or 2 teaspoons dried chervil
1 cup chopped scallions
⅔ cup heavy cream

1 Make the filling: Par-cook the potato slices for 3 minutes in a large pan of boiling, salted water and drain.
2 Preheat the oven to 400°F. Roll out slightly more than half the dough on a floured surface, and use it to line a greased 9 inch pie pan.
3 Arrange about one-third of the potato slices in the pie shell, season lightly with salt and pepper and sprinkle over about half the herbs and scallions. Cover with another third of the potato slices, season and sprinkle with the rest of the herbs and scallions, then cover with the remaining potato.
4 Beat the egg yolk with 1 tablespoon water and brush the dough edges. Roll out the rest of the dough to make a crust and cover the pie. Press edges together to seal well. Brush with the egg yolk and cut 4 small steam slits in the piecrust. Bake for 25 minutes, then reduce oven temperature to 350°F and cook for 20 minutes more.
5 Remove the pie from the oven and open the steam slits sufficiently with a sharp knife to take a small funnel. Pour one-fourth of the cream into each of the steam slits and return the pie to the oven for 10 minutes more, or until the crust is rich golden brown. Serve hot.

Slatted pie

Serves 6–8

¾ lb Puff pastry (see page 10)
1 egg, beaten, for glaze
FILLING
1 lb Jerusalem artichokes
2 tablespoons lemon juice
salt
2 tablespoons butter
2 tablespoons all-purpose flour
⅔ cup milk
3 tablespoons heavy cream
1 tablespoon lemon juice
½ teaspoon American mustard
2 tablespoons fresh chopped parsley
freshly ground black pepper
1 cup chopped cooked ham
1½ cups shredded Monterey Jack

1 Preheat the oven to 425°F.
2 Make the filling: Pare the artichokes and immediately put them in a bowl of water to which 1 tablespoon lemon juice has been added. Drain and add to a pan of lightly salted boiling water. Cook, covered, for 10 minutes until just tender. Strain and keep covered on kitchen paper towels until cold.
3 Melt the butter in a saucepan, stir in the flour and cook gently for 1–2 minutes. Gradually add the milk, stirring until the sauce comes to a boil and thickens. Off heat, stir in the heavy, cream, remaining lemon juice, mustard and parsley and season with salt and pepper. Mix in the ham and the cheese. Chop the artichokes and add to the sauce. Let cool.
4 Divide the pastry in half. Roll out one half to a 9 inch round and the other to a 10 inch round. Beat the egg with 1 teaspoon cold water.
5 Put the smaller pastry round onto a lightly greased baking sheet. Brush a border 1 inch wide with the beaten egg. Spread the cold filling over the dough, up to the border.
6 Fold the larger pastry round in half. Cut slats in the pastry, ½ inch apart, at right angles to the fold and to within 1 inch of the opposite rounded edge. Unfold the pastry carefully over a rolling pin and lift it over the filling. Press the edges together and neaten the strips over the filling.
7 Crimp the piecrust in wide scallops. Brush the dough with the egg.
8 Bake on the center shelf of the oven for 15 minutes. Lower the heat to 400°F and bake for 5–10 minutes more. Serve hot or cold.

Pizza turnover

Serves 4

¾ lb Basic pie dough (see page 10)
1 egg yolk, beaten, for glaze
FILLING
½ cup Ricotta cheese
1 cup cubed Italian salami
1 cup crumbled Mozzarella cheese
1 tablespoon olive oil
salt and freshly ground black pepper
TOMATO SAUCE
1 can (16 oz) tomatoes, drained
1 clove garlic, crushed
1 tablespoon chopped fresh basil or 1 teaspoon dried basil
⅓ cup olive oil
1 teaspoon sugar

1 Preheat the oven to 400°F. On a lightly floured surface roll out dough to a round 12 inches in diameter.
2 Put the Ricotta in a bowl and break it up with a fork. Mix in salami, Mozzarella and oil. Season well with salt and pepper.
3 Spoon filling onto half of the round of dough, leaving a 1 inch border. Fold the dough ovr to form a half moon shape. Pinch the dough edges together; seal the edges with a fork, and

then brush them with egg yolk.
4 Carefully transfer the turnover to a baking sheet. Bake for 35–40 minutes or until edges are golden.
5 While the turnover is baking, make the tomato sauce: Combine all the ingredients in a small saucepan. Bring to a boil and continue cooking over medium heat, uncovered, for 10–15 minutes, stirring occasionally. The oil should separate out from the tomatoes. Serve the sauce with the turnover.

Cabbage Koulibiaka

Serves 4

1 lb Savoy cabbage, coarse leaves and stems removed, sliced
¼ cup butter
1 onion, chopped
3 hard-cooked eggs, chopped
1 teaspoon dillweed
1 tablespoon minced fresh parsley
2 good pinches sugar
salt and freshly ground black pepper
¾ lb Puff pastry (see page 10)
1 egg, beaten, for glaze

1 Preheat the oven to 425°F. Line a baking sheet with foil.
2 Put the cabbage in a colander and slowly pour over a kettle of boiling water. Let stand for 2 minutes, until the cabbage is just cool enough to handle, then press the cabbage down with the back of a spoon in the colander to extract all the excess moisture.
3 Melt half the butter in a medium-size saucepan and cook the onion over moderate heat for 3 minutes, until soft. Add the cabbage, stir well, then cook over moderate heat for 5–6 minutes, stirring frequently, until the cabbage is cooked but still crisp. Remove from the heat and add the eggs, dillweed, parsley and sugar. Season well with salt and pepper.
4 Cut off just less than half the pastry, roll it out on a lightly floured surface and trim to a 12 × 6 inch rectangle. Lay it on prepared baking sheet. Pile cabbage filling onto the pastry, leaving a 1 inch border. Brush the border with beaten egg.
5 Roll out the remaining pastry and trim to a 13 × 8 inch rectangle. Lay the pastry over the filling, press the edges together to seal and crimp decoratively. Make 3 holes in the top of the pie and decorate with "leaves" made from pastry trimmings. Brush over with beaten egg, to glaze.
6 Bake in the oven for 25 minutes, until well risen and golden brown, then reduce the oven temperature to 375°F and bake for 15 minutes more.
7 Remove pie from oven. Melt remaining butter and pour it into pie by inserting a funnel into each hole. Serve at once, piping hot.

Mushroom & pimiento roll

Serves 4

¼ cup butter
1 cup minced onion
3 cups chopped button mushrooms
1 cup chopped drained canned pimientos
salt and freshly ground black pepper
¾ lb Puff pastry (see page 10)
1 egg, beaten, for glaze
⅔ cup dairy sour cream, to serve

1 Preheat the oven to 375°F.
2 Melt the butter in a large skillet, add the onion and sauté gently for about 5 minutes, until soft and lightly colored.
3 Add the mushrooms, stir well and cook gently for about 5 minutes, stirring occasionally, until all the liquid has evaporated.
4 Transfer the sautéed mixture to a large bowl, add the chopped pimientos and mix well. Season generously with salt and pepper, then let cool.
5 Meanwhile, roll out the pastry thinly on a lightly floured surface to a neat rectangle about 18 × 14 inches.

6 Drain the cooled mushroom mix, squeezing out excess moisture and spread over the pastry, leaving a pastry border all around of about ½ inch. Starting at 1 long edge, roll up the pastry. Gently press the roll to flatten the shape slightly, then tuck the ends in and brush with water so that they stick together.
7 Dampen a large baking sheet and, using 2 fish turners, carefully transfer the pastry roll to the sheet, join side down. Brush all over with the egg.
8 Bake for 25 minutes. Serve hot, cut in slices with sour cream.

Meat loaf package

Serves 6

1½ lb lean ground beef
1½ cups soft white bread crumbs
1 onion, minced
1 clove garlic, minced
⅔ cup dairy sour cream
2 eggs, beaten
salt and freshly ground black pepper
¼ cup butter
1½ cups thinly sliced mushrooms
½ teaspoon dried thyme
1 tablespoon white wine
¾ lb Puff pastry (see page 10)
beaten egg, to glaze
butter, for greasing

1 Preheat the oven to 350°F. Grease a roasting pan.
2 Put the beef, bread crumbs and half the onion in a bowl with the garlic. Mix in the sour cream, eggs and salt and pepper to taste. Transfer the mixture to the prepared roasting pan and form into a 7 × 3½ × 3 inch loaf shape.
3 Bake in the oven for 45 minutes, then remove from oven and let cool completely in the pan. Increase oven temperature to 425°F.
4 Melt the butter in a skillet, add the remaining onion and the mushrooms and sauté gently for 5 minutes. Stir in the thyme and wine, and cook for 5 minutes more. Season with salt and pepper. Using a slotted spoon, transfer to a bowl and set aside.
5 Roll out the pastry on a floured surface to a 15 × 12 inch rectangle. Brush edges with water.
6 Spoon the mushroom mixture over center of pastry. With 2 fish turners transfer meat loaf to center of pastry. Wrap loaf in pastry.
7 Invert onto moistened baking sheet, brush with egg and bake in the oven for 10 minutes. Lower oven temperature to 350°F and bake for 25 minutes more until crust is golden and filling cooked (cover with waxed paper if crust is overbrowning). Serve hot.

Sausage braid

Serves 6–8

1½ lb good-quality bulk pork sausage
3 tablespoons sweet pickle
1 tablespoon minced onion
2 teaspoons Jamaican mustard
1 teaspoon dried mixed herbs
¾ lb Puff pastry (see page 10)
1 egg, beaten
vegetable oil, for greasing
poppy seeds, for sprinkling

1 Put the bulk sausage into a bowl with the sweet pickle, onion, mustard and herbs. Mix well to combine.
2 Preheat the oven to 400°F and dampen a baking sheet.
3 Roll out the pastry on a floured surface to a 12 × 10 inch rectangle. Trim the edges then transfer to the baking sheet.
4 Lightly mark the rectangle in 3 lengthwise and spread the sausage-mix down the center section, forming it into a neat roll.

5 Make an equal number of diagonal cuts 1 inch apart along the uncovered pastry at each side to within ½ inch of the filling. Brush the pastry strips with egg and fold over the sausage to give a braid effect.
6 Brush the braid all over with beaten egg, sprinkle with poppy seeds then bake in the oven for 45 minutes or until the crust is golden brown. Cover with foil towards the end of cooking if overbrowning. Serve the braid warm or cold.

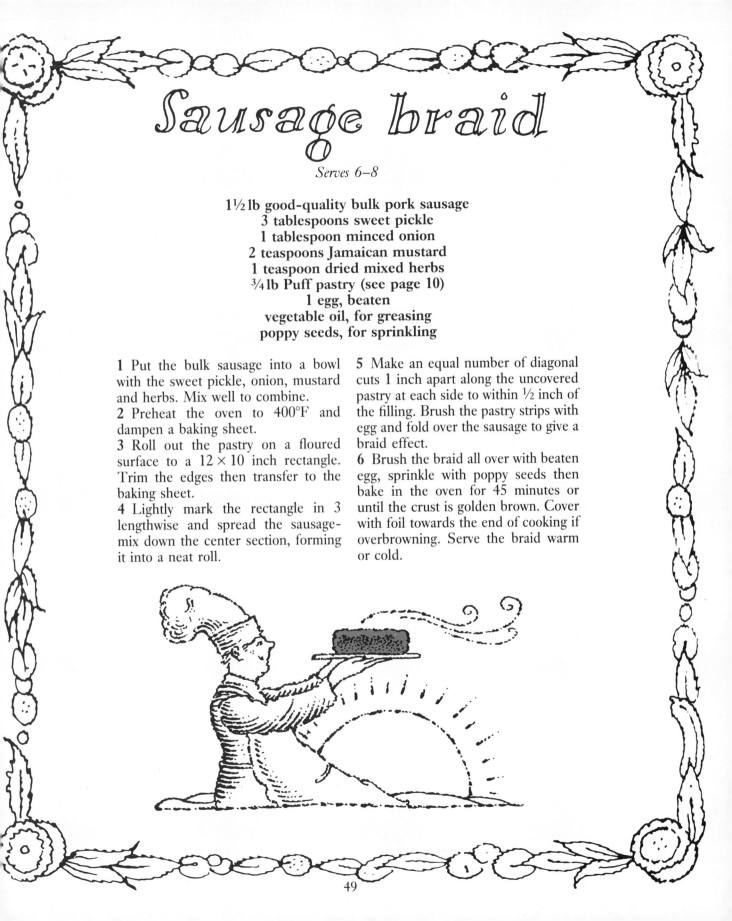

Greek lamb in a blanket

Serves 4

½ lb Puff pastry (see page 10)
beaten egg, for glaze
FILLING
½ lb ground lamb
1 eggplant, (about ½ lb), finely chopped
1 clove garlic, minced
½ cup soft white bread crumbs
1 egg, beaten
½ teaspoon dried oregano or mixed herbs
1 teaspoon chopped fresh mint
about ¼ teaspoon freshly grated nutmeg
½ cup crumbled Feta cheese
salt and freshly ground black pepper

1 Preheat the oven to 400°F.
2 Make the filling: In a bowl, mix together all the ingredients for the filling except the cheese. Season with salt and pepper to taste.
3 Roll pastry on a floured surface to a 13 × 7 inch rectangle. Reserve pastry trimmings.
4 Spoon half lamb mixture down center of the pastry to within 1 inch of the 2 short ends. Sprinkle the cheese on top and cover with remaining lamb mix. Brush the edges of the pastry with water. Seal the 2 long edges down the length of the loaf, then tuck in the short ends and seal thoroughly.
6 Dampen a baking sheet and carefully transfer the filled roll, join side down, to it. Brush with egg and cut 2 slashes on top.
7 Make decors from the pastry trimmings, brush the undersides with water and fix on the loaf, with some of the beaten egg, then brush all over with beaten egg. Bake in the oven for 35–40 minutes until filling is cooked through and crust is golden, covering the top with foil or waxed paper if it begins to overbrown. Transfer to a serving platter and serve hot or cold.

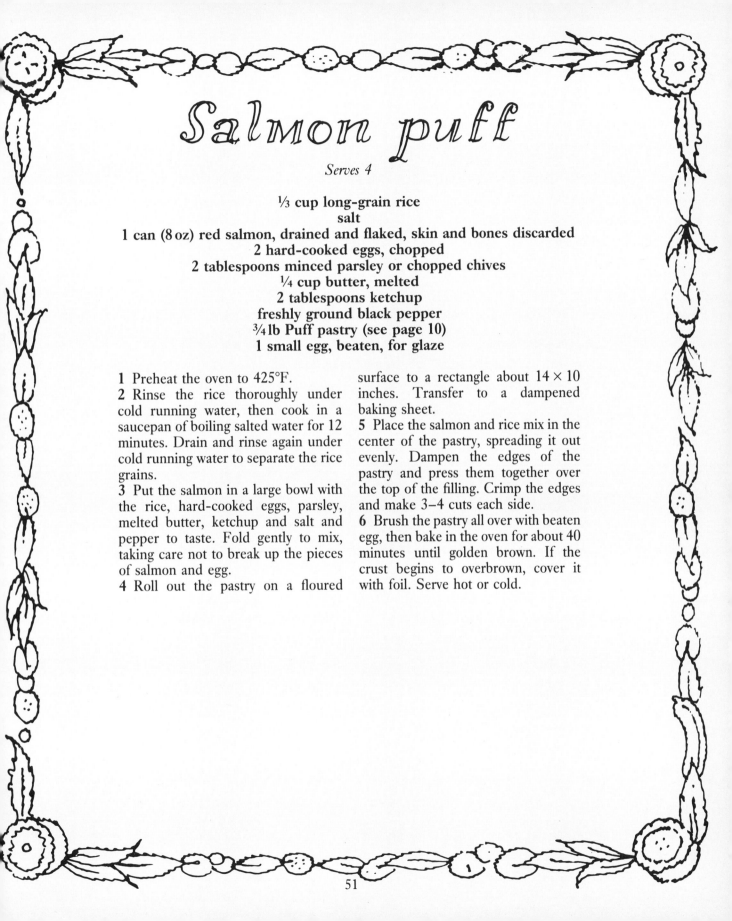

Salmon puff

Serves 4

⅓ cup long-grain rice
salt
1 can (8 oz) red salmon, drained and flaked, skin and bones discarded
2 hard-cooked eggs, chopped
2 tablespoons minced parsley or chopped chives
¼ cup butter, melted
2 tablespoons ketchup
freshly ground black pepper
¾ lb Puff pastry (see page 10)
1 small egg, beaten, for glaze

1 Preheat the oven to 425°F.
2 Rinse the rice thoroughly under cold running water, then cook in a saucepan of boiling salted water for 12 minutes. Drain and rinse again under cold running water to separate the rice grains.
3 Put the salmon in a large bowl with the rice, hard-cooked eggs, parsley, melted butter, ketchup and salt and pepper to taste. Fold gently to mix, taking care not to break up the pieces of salmon and egg.
4 Roll out the pastry on a floured surface to a rectangle about 14 × 10 inches. Transfer to a dampened baking sheet.
5 Place the salmon and rice mix in the center of the pastry, spreading it out evenly. Dampen the edges of the pastry and press them together over the top of the filling. Crimp the edges and make 3–4 cuts each side.
6 Brush the pastry all over with beaten egg, then bake in the oven for about 40 minutes until golden brown. If the crust begins to overbrown, cover it with foil. Serve hot or cold.

Individual Pies

This chapter has something for everyone — a pie for each and every occasion, filled with country goodness! There are individual top crust pies, like the super Steak pies cooked in a creamy rich crust — certain to impress at lunch or dinner; little open-faced pies such as our Summer salmon tarts, delicious when accompanied by a chilled white wine at a party or summer buffet; hearty pasties and turnovers, perfect for packing in lunchpails; and delicate puff pastry surprises, such as the Mushroom bites, served with a blue cheese dressing.

Pork turnovers

Serves 4

8 slices pork loin, cut 1½–1¾ inches thick
freshly ground black pepper
¾ lb Puff pastry (see page 10)
1 egg yolk
1 tablespoon cold water
STUFFING
⅓ cup dry white bread crumbs
3 tablespoons minced fresh parsley
1 tablespoon minced onion
finely grated rind of 1 lemon
2 teaspoons lemon juice
½ teaspoon ground ginger
1½ teaspoons mild curry powder
pinch of cayenne
3–4 tablespoons melted butter
celery salt or salt

1 Put the pork slices between 2 sheets of waxed paper and beat with a rolling pin until ¼ inch thick. Season the slices on both sides with black pepper.
2 Mix together all the stuffing ingredients, except the melted butter and salt. Add enough melted butter to bind the mixture and season to taste with celery salt and pepper.
3 Preheat the oven to 425°F.
4 Spread the stuffing mixture on 4 of the pork slices, to within ½ inch of the edges. Cover with the remaining slices, to make "sandwiches" with stuffing filling.
5 Cut the pastry in 4 equal pieces and roll out each piece on a floured surface to an 8–9 inch square. Trim the edges of each square. Mix the egg yolk with the cold water and brush the pastry squares with a little of this mixture, making sure you brush right to the edges of the squares.
6 Place a pork "sandwich" on one-half of each square, fold the pastry over and press the edges together to seal. Trim the edges to a semicircular shape, leaving a ¾ inch pastry border around the pork. Seal edges and crimp. Cut 3 small slits in the top of each turnover with a sharp knife.
7 With a fish turner transfer the turnovers to a dampened baking sheet and brush them all over with the remaining egg yolk mixture. Bake in the oven for 20–25 minutes, until deep golden brown. Serve the pork turnovers hot or cold.

Steak pies

Makes 6 small pies

½ cup all-purpose flour
1 teaspoon dry mustard
salt and freshly ground black pepper
2½ lb chuck steak, trimmed and cut in 1 inch cubes
¾ lb beef kidney, trimmed and cut in 1 inch cubes
¼–⅓ cup oil
1 large onion, minced
2 cups beef stock
1–2 tablespoons Worcestershire sauce
1–2 tablespoons minced fresh parsley
2 cups quartered mushrooms
beaten egg, for glaze
CREAM CRUST
3 cups all-purpose flour
good pinch of salt
½ cup diced butter
⅔ cup heavy cream

1 Put the flour in a plastic bag with the mustard, and season with salt and pepper. Add the cubes of steak and kidney and shake until well coated with flour.

2 Heat ¼ cup oil in a large saucepan, add a batch of meat and cook over moderate heat for about 5 minutes until browned on all sides. Remove with a slotted spoon and set aside. Cook remaining meat in the same way.

3 Lower the heat and add the onion to the pan, adding a little more oil if necessary. Sauté gently for 5 minutes until the onion is soft and lightly colored.

4 Gradually stir in the stock, then add the Worcestershire and bring to a boil, stirring. Return the meat to the pan, then lower the heat and add parsley.

Cover and simmer for 2 hours until the meat is tender. Off heat, add the mushrooms to the pan and allow the mixture to cool.

5 Meanwhile, make the cream crust: Sift the flour and salt into a bowl. Add the butter and rub it in until the mixture resembles coarse meal. Make a well in the center and pour in the cream. Using a round-bladed knife, gradually draw the flour mixture into the cream to form a smooth dough. Wrap and let stand in a cool place or the refrigerator for 30 minutes.

6 Preheat the oven to 400°F and select 6 individual 1½ cup pie dishes or ovenproof soup bowls.

7 Meanwhile, make the pie lids: Roll out the dough thinly on a lightly floured surface. Using one of the upturned pie dishes as a guide, cut out 6 rounds. Roll out trimmings, and cut in 4 strips, each ½ inch wide and long enough to fit around the rims of the pie dishes. Reserve strips, lids and trimmings.

8 Divide cooked steak and kidney among the 6 pie dishes, piling the meat high in the center to support dough.

9 Brush the rims of the pie dishes with water, then press the narrow strips of pastry all around each rim. Brush the strips with a little more water, then place the large rounds on top. Trim the edges of the dough, then seal and crimp.

10 Make leaves with the dough trimmings, brush the undersides with water and press on top of the pies. Make a steam slit in the center of each pie, then brush each crust with a little beaten egg.

11 Bake the pies in the oven for about 45 minutes or until the crusts are golden brown. Serve at once, straight from the pie dishes.

Frankfurter shells

Makes 4

1 tablespoon vegetable oil
1 small onion, minced
6 tablespoons drained canned whole kernel corn
1 tablespoon ketchup
1½ cups sliced frankfurters
salt and freshly ground black pepper
¾ lb Basic pie dough (see page 10)
1 egg, beaten, for glaze

1 Preheat the oven to 400°F.

2 Heat the oil in a saucepan. Sauté the onion gently for 10 minutes until browned. Add the canned corn, ketchup and the sliced frankfurters and season with salt and pepper to taste. Mix well and remove from the heat.

3 Roll out the dough. Invert a scallop shell or scalloped dish on the dough and use as a guide to cut scallop shapes, re-rolling the trimmings so that you cut 8 shapes in all. Then brush the edges with water. Reserve any dough trimmings for decors.

4 Divide the frankfurter filling equally among 4 dough half shells. Cover with the remaining dough half shells matching the edges carefully. Press them together. Decorate with trimmings, fixing them on with beaten egg.

5 Brush shells with beaten egg and carefully lift onto a baking sheet with a fish turner. Bake in the oven for about 20 minutes until golden brown and crisp underneath. Serve the frankfurter shells hot or cold.

Tongue pasties

Serves 4

1½ cups diced raw potato
salt and freshly ground black pepper
¾ cup butter
1 onion, chopped
½ lb cooked beef tongue, diced
1 egg, beaten
2½ cups self-rising flour
milk, for glaze
vegetable oil, for greasing

1 Bring the potatoes to a boil in salted water, lower the heat and cook for about 20 minutes until tender. Drain and mash thoroughly. Let potatoes cool for 10 minutes.

2 Preheat the oven to 400°F and lightly grease a baking sheet with vegetable oil.

3 Melt 2 tablespoons of the butter in a skillet. Add the onion and sauté gently for 10 minutes until browned. Drain thoroughly on kitchen paper towels.

4 Put ⅔ cup mashed potato in a bowl and add the onion, diced tongue and egg. Mix well and season to taste with salt and pepper.

5 Beat the remaining butter with the remaining potato until smooth and creamy. Gradually work in the flour and 1 teaspoon salt. Use a spoon to begin with, then work the mixture with your fingers when it is stiffer and nearly all the flour has been added.

6 Divide the dough in 4 pieces. Roll out each piece on a well-floured surface into a round about 8 inches in diameter.

7 Place one-fourth of the tongue mix on one-half of each round. Fold the dough over it to form a semicircle. Seal the edges by pinching them together with your fingers, prick around the top of each pasty and transfer to the baking sheet. Brush with a little milk, then bake in the oven for 30 minutes until golden brown. Serve the pasties hot or cold.

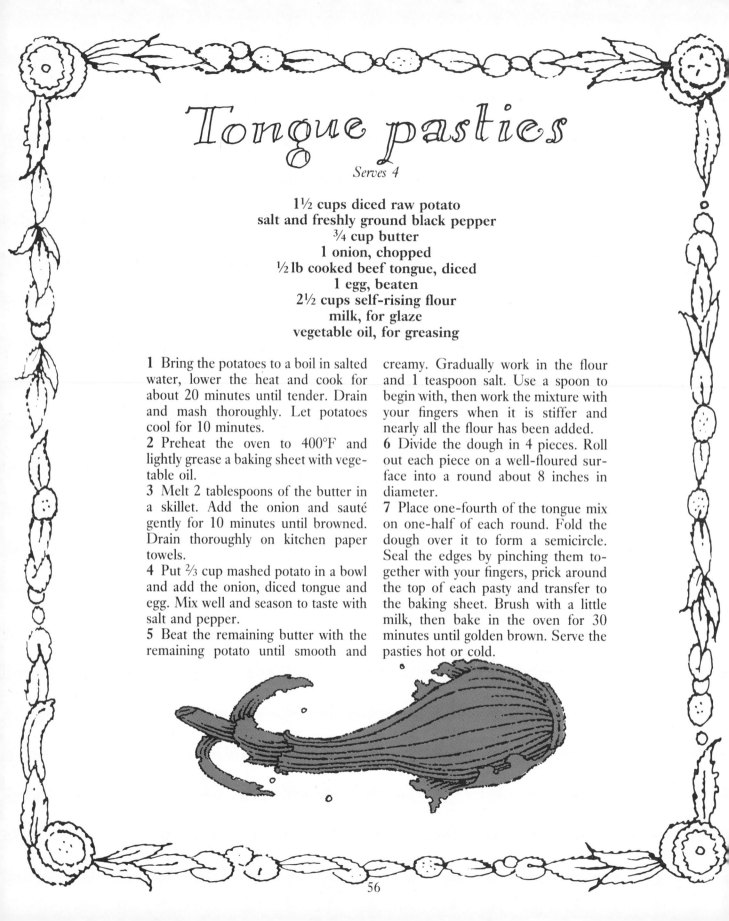

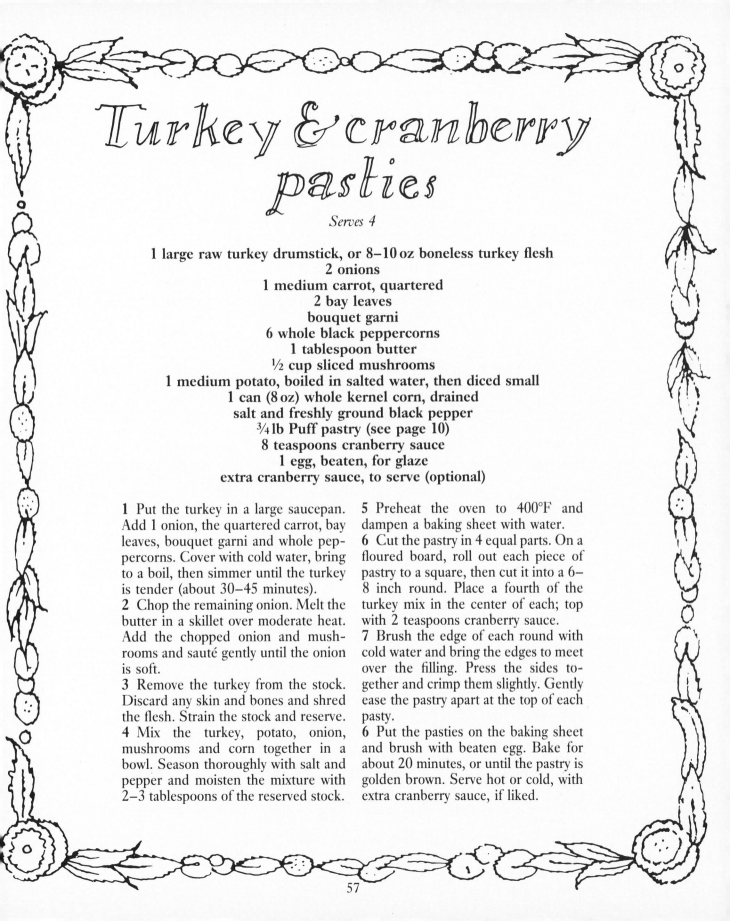

Turkey & cranberry pasties

Serves 4

1 large raw turkey drumstick, or 8–10 oz boneless turkey flesh
2 onions
1 medium carrot, quartered
2 bay leaves
bouquet garni
6 whole black peppercorns
1 tablespoon butter
½ cup sliced mushrooms
1 medium potato, boiled in salted water, then diced small
1 can (8 oz) whole kernel corn, drained
salt and freshly ground black pepper
¾ lb Puff pastry (see page 10)
8 teaspoons cranberry sauce
1 egg, beaten, for glaze
extra cranberry sauce, to serve (optional)

1 Put the turkey in a large saucepan. Add 1 onion, the quartered carrot, bay leaves, bouquet garni and whole peppercorns. Cover with cold water, bring to a boil, then simmer until the turkey is tender (about 30–45 minutes).

2 Chop the remaining onion. Melt the butter in a skillet over moderate heat. Add the chopped onion and mushrooms and sauté gently until the onion is soft.

3 Remove the turkey from the stock. Discard any skin and bones and shred the flesh. Strain the stock and reserve.

4 Mix the turkey, potato, onion, mushrooms and corn together in a bowl. Season thoroughly with salt and pepper and moisten the mixture with 2–3 tablespoons of the reserved stock.

5 Preheat the oven to 400°F and dampen a baking sheet with water.

6 Cut the pastry in 4 equal parts. On a floured board, roll out each piece of pastry to a square, then cut it into a 6–8 inch round. Place a fourth of the turkey mix in the center of each; top with 2 teaspoons cranberry sauce.

7 Brush the edge of each round with cold water and bring the edges to meet over the filling. Press the sides together and crimp them slightly. Gently ease the pastry apart at the top of each pasty.

6 Put the pasties on the baking sheet and brush with beaten egg. Bake for about 20 minutes, or until the pastry is golden brown. Serve hot or cold, with extra cranberry sauce, if liked.

Harvest pork pies

Serves 6

1 lb pork tenderloin, finely diced
5 bacon slices, finely diced
½ cup chopped walnuts
½ cup minced mushrooms (including stems)
1 tart apple, pared and shredded
1 cup soft white bread crumbs
2 teaspoons Worcestershire sauce
¼ teaspoon freshly grated nutmeg
½ teaspoon salt
plenty of freshly ground black pepper
1 teaspoon dried thyme
1 egg, lightly beaten
lard, for greasing
beaten egg, for glaze
6 tablespoons dry sherry
sprigs of parsley, for garnish
WHOLEWHEAT PIE DOUGH
2 cups Graham flour
2 cups all-purpose flour
½ teaspoon salt
½ cup leaf lard
½ cup butter or margarine
about ½–¾ cup ice water

1 Make the dough: Sift the flours and salt into a large bowl, rubbing through any lumps, then tip in the bran left in the sifter. Cut in the leaf lard and butter, and rub in with the fingertips until the mixture resembles coarse meal. Stir in the water with a round-bladed knife, draw the mixture together to form a dough and knead lightly. Wrap in plastic wrap and refrigerate for 30 minutes.

2 Meanwhile, make the filling: Put the pork in a large bowl with the bacon, walnuts, mushrooms, apple, bread crumbs, Worcestershire, nutmeg, salt and plenty of black pepper. Stir in the thyme and beaten egg and mix thoroughly.

3 Preheat the oven to 400°F and lightly grease 1 or 2 baking sheets with lard. Roll out one-fourth of the dough on a lightly floured surface to ⅛ inch thickness. Cut out a 7 inch square and set aside; reserve trimmings. Cut out 3 more squares with the remaining three-fourths of the dough, then use the reserved trimmings to make 2 more dough squares.

4 To fill the pies, pile one-sixth of the filling into the center of each square, pressing it into a pyramid shape. Brush the edges of the dough square with water, then bring the corners together over the filling. Pinch the edges firmly together, leaving ¾ inch wide gap at the top, then cut out decorative leaves from the trimmings. Brush the undersides with water and fix the leaves to top of piecrusts to decorate. Transfer the pies to the greased baking sheets with a fish turner and brush all over with beaten egg.

5 Bake the pies in the oven for 30 minutes, then lower the oven temperature to 350°F and bake for 20–30 minutes more, until they are golden brown. Just before serving, pour 1 tablespoon of sherry into each pie through the hole in the top, then put a sprig of parsley in each. Serve hot.

Summer salmon tarts

Serves 4

½ lb Basic pie dough (see page 10)
1 can (4 oz) red salmon, drained and flaked, skin and bones discarded
1 small onion, minced
2 teaspoons chopped chives
⅔ cup plain yogurt
2 eggs
⅔ cup milk
salt and freshly ground black pepper

1 Preheat the oven to 400°F.
2 Roll out the dough thinly on a lightly floured surface. Cut out four 5 inch rounds, using an inverted saucer or small plate as a guide.
3 Press each round into a 4 inch small deep tart pan. Ease the dough into the base and press into the side. Trim off any excess dough and prick the tart shells with a fork. Cover and refrigerate for 15 minutes.
4 Meanwhile, make the filling: Mix the salmon, onion and chives together in a bowl. In a pitcher, beat the yogurt and eggs together until smooth, then gradually stir in the milk. Season with salt and pepper.
5 Divide salmon mix equally among tart shells, spreading it evenly. Pour the yogurt mix over the salmon, filling each shell almost to the top.
6 Place the tart pans on a baking sheet and bake in the oven for 30–40 minutes until golden.
7 Transfer to a serving platter and serve warm or cold.

Kidney, sausage & mushroom pies

Serves 4

8 lamb kidneys
½ lb mini pork sausage links
2 tablespoons butter
1 tablespoon vegetable oil
about 20 whole pearl onions
1 tablespoon wholewheat flour
about 1¼ cups beef stock
¾ cup red wine
½ lb whole button mushrooms
pinch of dried thyme
salt and freshly ground black pepper
¾ lb Puff pastry (see page 10)
1 egg, beaten, for glaze

1 Prepare the kidneys: Halve them lengthwise and snip out all the white cores. Slice each kidney half in 3 pieces. Twist each mini sausage in the center, then cut in half.

2 Melt the butter with the oil in a large skillet and sauté the onions over gentle heat until they are soft and lightly colored.

3 Raise the heat, add the kidneys and sausage to the pan and cook for about 10 minutes until browned. Remove the kidneys, sausage and onions from the pan with a slotted spoon and reserve.

4 Sprinkle the flour into the pan juices and cook for 1–2 minutes, stirring constantly. Gradually add the stock and red wine and bring to a boil, stirring so that the sauce is smooth.

5 Return the kidneys, sausage and onions to the pan, and add the mushrooms. Add the thyme and salt and pepper to taste, then cover and simmer for 15–20 minutes.

6 Preheat the oven to 400°F.

7 Meanwhile, roll out the pastry on a floured surface to a 16 × 14 inch rectangle. Using an upturned 1½ cup ovenproof soup bowl as a guide, cut the rectangle in 4 rounds. Roll out trimmings and cut in 4 strips each ½ inch wide and long enough to fit around the rims of the soup bowls.

8 Add a little more stock to the kidney mixture if it seems too thick, then bring to a boil again. Divide the mixture equally among the 4 soup bowls, brush the rims of the bowls with water, then press the pastry strips onto them.

9 Brush the strips with more water and place the rounds of pastry over the filling.

10 Press the edges of pastry together with your thumb or a fork, then cut off any surplus. Crimp the edges.

11 Brush the pastry with the beaten egg, then decorate the piecrusts with leaves made from any pastry trimmings, fixing them with more egg.

Make a small steam slit in the center.

12 Put the bowls on a baking sheet and bake in the oven for 10 minutes. Reduce the temperature to 350°F and bake for 10–15 minutes more until the pastry is puffed up and golden brown. Serve hot.

Individual watercress pies

Makes 4

½ quantity Rich pie dough (see page 42)
green food coloring
beaten egg or milk, for glaze
FILLING
2 bunches watercress, finely chopped
2 eggs, beaten
2 tablespoons melted butter
freshly grated nutmeg
salt and freshly ground black pepper

1 Preheat the oven to 375°F.

2 Divide dough into 9 equal pieces. With lightly floured hands, roll 8 pieces into balls. On a lightly floured surface, roll pieces into rounds 4½ inches in diameter.

3 Line four individual pie pans with dough rounds. Mix the filling ingredients in a bowl and season well with nutmeg, salt and freshly ground black pepper.

4 Divide the filling among the pie shells and bake, uncovered, for 15 minutes or until the filling has completely set.

5 Remove from the oven, dampen edges of 4 remaining dough rounds with water and place on top of the filling. Press the edges together and seal them quickly with the prongs of a floured fork.

6 Roll out remaining dough and use for leaves. Dampen undersides with water and fix to piecrusts. Make a small slit in center of each pie and color the leaves by painting them with food coloring. Brush the rest of the dough with beaten egg.

7 Return the pies to the oven and bake for 20 minutes more, or until crusts are cooked through and golden.

8 Let pies cool for a few minutes, then transfer to a wire rack. Serve warm or cold.

Mushroom bites & blue cheese dressing

Serves 4

12 cup mushrooms
½ lb Puff pastry (see page 10)
1 tablespoon butter
½ teaspoon dried marjoram
freshly ground black pepper
1 egg, lightly beaten
CHEESE DRESSING
3 tablespoons blue cheese
⅔ cup plain yogurt
2 scallions, finely sliced
salt and freshly ground black pepper

1 Trim the mushroom stems level with the caps, then mince the stems and reserve.

2 Roll out the pastry thinly on a lightly floured surface. Then, using a 3 inch fluted round cutter, cut out 24 rounds.

3 Place one mushroom, stem side up, on each of 12 pastry rounds. Put a small knob of butter, a pinch of marjoram and a sprinkling of salt and pepper on each mushroom.

4 Brush the edges of each mushroom-topped pastry round with beaten egg, then place a second round of pastry on top. Bring together the pastry edges, pressing well to seal. Crimp the edges.

5 Dampen 2 baking sheets and transfer the puffs to them. Cover the puffs with plastic wrap and refrigerate them for 15 minutes.

6 Preheat the oven to 425°F.

7 Meanwhile, make the cheese dressing: Crumble the cheese into a serving bowl, add a little yogurt and mix together with a fork until fairly smooth. Stir in the remaining yogurt, reserved mushroom stems and half the scallions. Sprinkle the remaining scallions on top of the sauce, cover with plastic wrap and refrigerate.

8 Brush the tops of the puffs with the remaining beaten egg, then bake in the oven for 10–15 minutes until well-risen and golden brown.

9 Pile the hot puffs onto a warm serving platter and serve with the chilled sauce passed separately.

Spicy vegetable pies

Makes 12

¾ lb Basic pie dough (see page 10)
FILLING
¼ cup olive oil
1 onion, minced
3 cloves garlic, minced (optional)
1½ cups diced zucchini
1 sweet red pepper, seeded and diced
⅓ cup tomato paste
½ teaspoon ground cumin
4 tablespoons chopped cilantro
few drops of hot pepper sauce
salt and freshly ground black pepper
1 egg, beaten, for glaze

1 Make the filling: Heat the oil in a large skillet, add the onion and garlic, if using, and sauté gently for 5 minutes until the onion is soft and lightly colored.

2 Add the diced zucchini and the red pepper and continue to cook for 2 minutes more, stirring the vegetables with a wooden spoon.

3 Stir in the tomato paste, cumin, cilantro, hot pepper sauce, and salt and pepper to taste. Continue to cook for 4 minutes more, stirring constantly, then remove from the heat and let cool for 10 minutes.

4 Preheat the oven to 350°F.

5 Roll out the dough very thinly on a lightly floured surface and cut out 12 rounds with a 3½ inch cutter and 12 rounds with a 3 inch cutter. Use larger rounds to line 12 deep muffin pans.

6 Divide the filling among the pie shells. Brush the edges of the remaining dough rounds with water, and place on top of filled pie shells. Press the edges of the lids to seal, then prick the tops.

7 Brush the top of each pie with beaten egg to glaze and bake in the oven for 30 minutes until the crusts are golden. Serve hot or cold.

Index